Vol. 3

Snowbird Christmas

Holiday Stories to
Warm Your Heart

Edited by Nancy L. Quatrano

Print ISBN: 978-0-9903419-5-6

Editing contributed by Cheryl Johnson-Konrad, Judy Leigh Peters, Nancy Quatrano, Jonni Anderson

Interior, front and back cover design by Jonni Anderson and Nancy Quatrano

Interior layout and pagination by Jonni Anderson (www.jonnianderson.com / StarwatchCreations.com)

Interior, front and back cover design by Jonni Anderson and Nancy Quatrano

WC Publishing
AN ON-TARGET WORDS COMPANY
386-546-5164
4625 Cedar Ford Blvd.
Hastings, FL 32145
ontargetwords.com/wc-publishing

Contents

Contents, Cont'd

NOVELETTES

From the Editor

Dear Reader,

Wow, what an exciting volume we have put together for you this year! Poetry, short stories and some longer stories called novelettes, all share these covers this year. Don't know exactly what a novelette is? That's a story shorter than a novella and too long to be a short story. And this year, we've got two of those!

You will laugh and cry, sit on the edge of your seat, and enjoy many good old-fashioned memories, some of which you'll recognize. I can't thank all these talented authors enough for their generosity in sharing these stories with us all. Where possible, I have included either website or email links for each author and I hope you'll take the time to let them know if you enjoyed their contribution to your holiday season. Or, you can let me know and I'll pass your email along to them.

As always, we wish you a very Merry Christmas, one filled with happy memories, laughter, and peace. Whether your holiday is Hanukkah, Christmas, Kawanza or other, the blessings available are the same for us all. Be sure to claim your share!

Best wishes, always.

Nancy Quatrano, Editor

POETRY

Christmas Eve at Our House

Harry E. Mann

Christmas time at our house,
when I was just a boy,
Was a season almost magic,
transformed by hope and joy.

Thanksgiving past, now carols
sweetly filled the air,
And rooms at school were trimmed
for a holiday affair.

In the crowded five-and-dime
kids from every class
Sought gifts for just a dollar,
neither more nor less.

At night the Christmas lights
would glow above the street.
Their reds and greens would guide
the weary shoppers' feet.

Some purchased gifts
whose price was very dear.
Others spent just pennies
hoarded throughout the year.

All hurried home on wearied feet
made light with Christmas cheer
To warming hearth and those we loved
and friends we held so dear.

Some days before we cut
a tree from out the wood
And garnished it with tinsel
in the corner where it stood.

I remember our house,
a large home made of wood,
A crude, unfinished eyesore
on the corner where it stood.

The downstairs ceiling
was the second-story floor,
And the roof of tin upstairs
sprang leaks when rain would pour.

Our only heat a stove
of one by two by three
Would quickly roast one side
while the other side would freeze.

I must have cut a million logs,
or maybe even more,
To feed that hungry monster
crouching on the floor

Christmas Eve at our house
around that cast-iron stove,
We sat while Mama read to us
how good and evil strove.

We heard the angel's message,
"Hail to thee, Most Fair!
You'll bear God's Son, Messiah,
David's righteous Son.

We heard how Joseph trembled
at what would seem to be
A cause of darkest scandal
at Christ's nativity.

We envisioned Mary
riding on an ass
Over rugged mountains
and through a narrow pass.

Into crowded Bethlehem
she rode at end of day,
Swollen, sore, and weary
as Joseph led the way.

The village inn was full;
so were the guest-rooms too!
The Virgin's pains came quickly
and the host was filled with rue.

"It isn't very much,"
he hesitantly said,
"But my stable offers shelter
and my manger an infant bed."

Soon the air was filled
with the Holy Infant's cries,
And the song of a thousand angels
sent from paradise.

"Peace on earth," they sang,
"goodwill to all mankind;
your Savior in a manger
shall be the heavenly sign."

The Christ, the Lord, all wrapped
in swaddling clothes they found,
And moved to awesome reverence
they knelt upon the ground.

The Shepherds left rejoicing
and spread the news around,
While Mary pondered everything
with thoughts that were profound.

Mama read how wise men
rode for months on end
To bring rich gifts to Jesus
and visit with his kin.

The bright star led the Magi
beyond the palace door
To Joseph's humble cottage
where Mary swept the floor.

They came and worshiped Christ,
went home another way,
Warned by angel vision
that Herod longed to slay.

"No other son of David,
not even one divine,"
Shouted raging Herod,
"shall have this throne of mine!"

"Kill all the village babes
beneath the age of two!
Let none escape the sword,
or I shall kill you too."

The cruel soldiers slew
every little child,
And streets ran with blood
from jealousy so vile.

Into ancient Egypt
the Holy Family fled
Before the evil ruler,
just a step ahead.

Sustained by gifts of wise men
of gold, frankincense, and myrrh,
They passed the days in safety
'til the angel brought God's word,

"Go home to Israel;
the evil king is dead."
And by God's Holy Spirit
into Nazareth they were led.

Mom gently closed the book
and reverently bowed her head.
"Let's give God thanks for Jesus,
and for Christmas love," she said.

"Oh, God, our thanks for Jesus
who fills us all with joy,
We pledge renewed commitment
his teachings to employ."

"Let all his holy goodness
secure our home in love
Until the day he calls us
to our mansion up above."

"Let's turn out the lights,"
my little brother said,
"And watch the lighted tree
before we go to bed."

As we sat in darkened room,
the softly glowing lights
Cast a spell of magic
o'er that special night.

The light of fire escaped
the glowing cast-iron stove
And reflected in linoleum
the warmth of human love.

The logs that burned were gathered
by Daddy's toil and sweat,
And the crude walls that sheltered us
were Daddy's very best.

The front door opened wide
and Daddy staggered in,
Laden down with presents
from all our kith and kin.

"Merry Christmas to all!" he cried,
full of Christmas cheer,
Lubricated, sometimes,
with too much Christmas beer.

The brightly-wrapped packages
were placed with loving care
Around the new-cut tree
whose fragrance filled the air.

"Off to bed," Mom said,
kissing us goodnight.
"Santa only comes
when eyes are shut fast-tight."

Hugs and kisses over,
we scampered up the stairs
To crawl beneath the covers
and say our childish prayers.

"Now I lay me down to sleep,
I pray the Lord my soul to keep.
If I should die before I wake,
I pray thee, Lord, my soul to take."

The cold wind blew and whistled
all that large house through,
But we were warm and comfy
'neath quilts of pink and blue.

We dreamed of Santa Claus,
reindeer, sleigh, and toys,
And hoped he wouldn't think
that we'd been naughty boys.

We hoped he'd be like Jesus,
forgiving all our sins,
Who loved us so he died for us
and rose to life again.

We drifted off to sleep,
excitement overcome
With sweet refreshing slumber,
the gift of God's own love.

Christmas Eve at our house,
when I was just a boy,
Was radiant with God's own love,
transformed by hope and joy.

About the Author

The Rev. Dr. Harry Mann is a retired United Methodist minister. He began his writing career by writing a weekly sermon for thirty-five years. This poem, was first written in 1983. The three books in the Carroll Family Saga, entirely fiction, were inspired by a real family of his acquaintance. It took over forty years, writing part-time, to finish the three books, two of which can be purchased at Amazon. He and his wife Pamela live in St. Augustine, Florida. Email Harry at harrymann@bellsouth.net

Crystal Christmas Bell

Karen Elaine Ringquist

Crystal Christmas bell rings in memories
of the past and present.
Every Christmas morning the bell rings,
my memories of beautiful blue eyes–
awake and sliding down the hall he goes!
Christmas angel sits gingerly on the tree,
smiling at our family.
The holidays in our family are a spiritual time,
time to love and celebrate being together.
Treasuring the memories of the past brings tears of joy.
Grandma Dyer would prepare sweet potato casserole,
passed under my nose,
with great delight–on the table it goes!
We hold onto the joy of those who left us long ago!
Memories of past Christmases melt my heart;
my son opening his gifts under the tree.
Christmas day, all his shiny new toy trucks
lined in a row!
Memories of beautiful blue eyes, frolicking
through the rolling green.

Now a man. May God hold him, in his hands!
Ahh, Sweet Sammie, our brown eyed,
short hair black daschund –
In her quest for food,
running around the Christmas tree,
Her sweet nose smelling the scent,
on each package, as she goes.
Memories abound, as the Christmas Bell
is tucked away every year,
in its special corner in Grandma's hutch.
Is it waiting for the special day to come,
to ring in past memories and joy?
To ring in happiness of the present holiday season?
My mom's picture, proudly sits on that hutch,
by the dove of peace.
May your hearts melt with tenderness
this Christmas day....
Savor the memories, taste the spice in life.
This Christmas day we are together in our hearts!

About the Author

Karen Ringquist submitted this Christmas poem from her home in the state of Washington. It is her only published work. A wife, mother, writer and realtor, Karen and her husband passed away in August. She was beloved by her family and friends, and her Christmas joy will be sorely missed this year.

Memories of Christmas Past

Deborah Spellen

Putting up the tree,
wrapping lights around it with glee.
The balls, some antiques, some new.
glow with an expectant hue.

A small village takes shape,
Houses Granddad made.
Dirt from the yard fashion roads.
Soon Santa will bring presents by the load.

The aroma of food cooking fills the air.
Tonight a feast and all will be there.
Children too excited to eat,
they dream of Christmas treats.

A family sits around the table,
fish, vegetables, gravy from the ladle
They do this every year,
laughter and singing we do hear.
Dinner over, kids run to the tree.
Now, they cry with glee.
"Open the presents," one by one.
It's Christmas Eve and it has come!

About the Author

Deborah is a gifted poet and has been a fan-fiction aficionado for many years. Her poetry has been in several publications over the years and we are delighted that she has shared her work with us in *Snowbirds!*

SHORT STORIES

The Hanukkah Bear

John Culson Boles

As I was making breakfast, my six-year-old daughter, Sarah, walked in and tugged on my apron.

"Mommy, today is the day they're giving away toys downtown. Remember?" she said, with a pleading look.

"Sarah, the fact that a lot of caring people donate toys so that underprivileged children can have a happy holiday is a wonderful thing. But those are meant to be Christmas presents, and you know that we don't celebrate Christmas."

The look on her face told me she wasn't ready to take "no" for an answer. "I know, Mommy, but they are for Hanukkah presents too. Look, this paper says so." Sarah reached into her pocket and handed me a flyer about the big toy giveaway at the civic center.

"See, it says Christmas, Kwanzaa, and Hanukkah gifts." Sarah looked at me with big brown eyes that could melt the hardest resolve.

"Well, I see it says that, but," I paused as I tried to figure out how to explain. "These toys are for underprivileged children, boys and girls from families that can't afford to buy presents for the holidays."

"But, Mommy, you said that we probably couldn't afford presents this year." Sarah chose her words as carefully as a bright six-year-old could. "Since Daddy lost his job and was out of work so long, you said there just isn't enough money this year. Doesn't that make us underprivileged?"

"We're just going through a rough time right now, sweetie. Things will get better. I promise you that." As I uttered those words, I also said a silent prayer that my words would come true, sooner rather than later.

Sarah thought for a moment, her smile waning for no more than an instant. "But, wouldn't it be okay for me to get just one present? It doesn't have to be anything fancy. Just one, please, Mommy. I won't ask for anything else, I promise."

There were those eyes again. How could I refuse such a heartfelt request?

"All right, sweetheart. We'll go down and see if we can find you one present for Hanukkah."

Sarah hugged me so tightly I could barely breathe. "Oh, thank you, Mommy! Thank you, so much!"

An hour later, Sarah and I entered the civic center that was lined with table after table of every type of toy imaginable. I looked down at my daughter and saw her face light up in wonder.

Holding her hand, I said, "Let's see if we can find something you like, simple though, nothing fancy or real expensive, okay?"

"Okay."

As we walked along the rows of tables, Sarah scanned the huge assortment of gifts. Suddenly, she stopped in her tracks and squeezed my hand. I glanced down at her to see an expression of absolute joy.

"What is it, Sarah? What do you see?"

"Down there, at the end." Sarah pointed to a table about fifty feet away. "The bear. Do you see it, Mommy?

He's so beautiful."

I followed her gaze and saw an enormous teddy bear nearly as tall as Sarah, and it appeared to have the most luxuriously thick fur I've ever seen on a stuffed toy. Sarah began walking again; this time her pace quickened as we approached the table. We were about six feet away when another girl and a boy both grabbed the bear at the same time.

"I saw it first!" the boy insisted.

"No you didn't. I saw it first, it's mine!" The girl tried to wrestle the bear away from him.

"Let go, it's mine!" the boy said loudly as he wrenched it away from the girl. Once the bear was in his arms, the boy inspected it more closely and his avarice turned to disgust.

"Aw, it's messed up!" With that, the boy threw the bear to the ground, turned, and stomped away. The girl reached down to pick up her prize but stopped in her tracks as she noticed what the boy had seen.

"Yuck," the girl exclaimed as she turned and walked away.

One of the event's volunteers walked over, picked up the bear, and brushed it off. Sarah and I approached him.

"Excuse me, sir," I spoke to the man. "Do you have any idea why those children didn't want this bear?"

The man smiled sadly and said, "Some of the toys have an imperfection. The company can't sell it, so they donate it, as a tax write-off I assume. Those two kids probably didn't want it because of this." The man tilted the bear toward us so we could see the top of its head. There was a round bald spot about four inches in diameter.

Sarah exclaimed, "Look, Mommy, it's a Jewish bear!"

Sure enough, the furless circle did give the appearance that the bear had on a yarmulke, the small skullcap that Jewish men wear at services. The volunteer saw the twinkle in Sarah's eyes and asked her if she would like the plush toy.

"Oh, yes sir, I love him."

The man handed the fuzzy giant to Sarah and said, "It looks like this bear has a new home, and a new little girl to love."

Sarah hugged the big, beautiful bear and said, "Thank you."

As we walked out into the bright Florida sunshine, a chilly breeze began blowing through our hair. I looked down at Sarah and relished the loving smile on her face as I realized this was going to be a wonderful holiday for our family after all; all four of us: Sarah, her dad, me, and the Hanukkah Bear.

About the Author

John Culson Boles is a professional editor, writing coach, script doctor, and award-winning writer with over thirty years of experience. Many of the authors and screenwriters in his popular critique workshops have seen their work win competitions, be published, broadcast, or produced for the screen. John teaches creative writing courses at the University of North Florida as well as Screenwriting and Film courses at Jacksonville University.

Can It Really Be Christmas Without Snow?

Skye Taylor

That was the question I'd been asking myself ever since the Peace Corps had managed to provide a small turkey for the group of volunteers stationed on my island to prepare for our Thanksgiving feast. Nothing that we had with the turkey even remotely replicated anything any of us considered traditional back home. But we'd done our best with the local options available on our little tropical paradise in the South Pacific.

Since none of us had dwellings big enough to host dinner for all of us together, one enterprising woman in our group had secured the use of a lovely little deck that hung out over the harbor. The deck was part of a small eatery and bar that only opened after four in the afternoon for the nighttime crowd of expats and yachties who frequented the very un-Tongan spots along the waterfront. We laughed and enjoyed our mostly un-American dinner as we celebrated the holiday half way around the world from everything we knew.

At one point, I had to run up to the Peace Corps office to retrieve something I'd promised to one of the other volunteers. I pushed through the swinging doors and ran up the stairs to the bustling main street of our small but busy little island. The fact that it was not a holiday in Tonga struck home as I hurried along a street filled with people going about their usual Thursday business. When I returned, trotted back down the stairs and through the doors, I stepped back onto the deck and was amazed at the change in atmosphere. It really did feel like Thanksgiving.

Now Christmas was approaching. Tongans do celebrate Christmas, but mostly as a religious holiday and without the commercial trappings Americans are accustomed to. Not only that, I had tickets to fly to an even more remote island aboard a tiny twelve-passenger airplane to spend the holiday with two other volunteers. The island had plane service only once a week and a ship came once a month – most of the time. There were three villages on the island, and life there was very, very remote from the modern day world.

Because eggs were hard to come by on Mark's remote outpost, I boarded the plane with a waffled cardboard flat of thirty eggs, which I held on my lap for the entire flight. It was part of my offering for our holiday together. Sandeep, who was stationed in the capital on the biggest island in the country, had flown up the week before and he'd promised to bring things I hadn't tasted in months even on my island that made some effort to cater to the needs of visiting yachts. It would be an interesting week.

I come from New England. A totally different climate, where a Christmas without snow was rare. Bing Crosby's "I'm Dreaming of a White Christmas" was my theme song that year. Mark was from New England, too, but Sandeep hailed from Texas so at least one of us was used to hot sultry Christmases. None of us really knew what to expect.

The plane came in low over coral reefs and sparkling turquoise water, bounced along a grassy airstrip and came to stop just a short distance from a low rail fence that kept the crowd of local folks who'd come to meet the plane from surging onto the runway. I stepped out of the plane into the brilliant, hot sunlight of Tongatapu and down the short flight of steps. Mark and Sandeep waved to me from the other side of the fence wearing Santa hats. I laughed so hard I almost dropped the eggs.

Maybe it would feel like Christmas after all.

Christmas Eve we donned our traditional Tongan finery and attended church as did everyone else on the island. The Midnight mass was a familiar part of my Christmas custom. The ringing of church bells all over the island was not, but it was beautiful and memorable.

Mark had brought a sprouting coconut home back in March when he first came to the island and it was now a slender but healthy shoot about four feet tall with a delicate spray of leaves which he'd festooned with beads of the sort you might find at Mardi Gras in New Orleans. That was our Christmas tree.

On Christmas morning, Mark produced stockings for each of us that his mother had filled and shipped months back. I hope to meet that woman someday – her thoughtfulness was a wonderful reminder of family back home and the traditions we grew up with. I still have the little Santa figurine she put in the top of mine. I have no recollection ten years later of the gifts we exchanged between us, but somehow we'd managed to find things each of us could use and appreciate. Opening gifts is always fun however small the offering.

There was no Christmas dinner to compare with the Thanksgiving feast, but somehow it didn't matter. Mark had fresh eggs for breakfast and that was a treat. Sandeep had brought chocolate and that was a treat for all of us. There is no electricity on Mark's island which ruled out anything that required refrigeration, but somehow Mark had mastered the art of creating pizza that didn't require real cheese. Pizza for Christmas was another new experience.

When dinner was done we went for a walk. December is mid-summer in Tonga and the temps were well into the nineties. Mark led us up to the top of a ridge that runs down the length of the island where we had a spectacular view of Tongatapu, the reefs that ringed it and the beautiful blue ocean beyond that. We slid and scrambled back down the steep hillside and back onto the road with considerable difficulty and emerged hot, sweaty and layered with fine sandy dirt. But Mark had a plan for that, too.

Within sight of his little house was a fissure in the ground that opened into a deep fresh water spring as big as a public pool back home. It was a favorite hangout for Mark and all the local kids and a few of the adults as well. Tongans don't own bathing suits so we swam in our clothes. Not that leaving bathing suits behind helped us blend in very well, our Caucasian skin pale in spite of our tans when compared to the rich dark complexions of the Polynesian Tongans. But we did try to honor the local conservative culture.

The Via (which means water or liquid in Tongan) was cool and refreshing and I could have stayed there for the rest of the day. At one end, the spring pushed under the overhang into a cave and big fish shared the water with us. I have a photo of Mark sitting on the bottom of the Via with fish swimming all around him. It was a delightfully different way to spend a Christmas afternoon.

As darkness fell and the day began to draw to a close, we munched on leftover pizza and chocolate and settled in to play cards. We wore our little headlamps to light up our hands which worked really good until the heat from the headlight began to bake our foreheads. Amazing how hot those little lamps can feel when it's 80 degrees. Sandeep had brought some CDs and we listened to music on a battery-driven player, some traditional Christmas music, some soundtracks that were new, at least to us.

When the game was over and the night as dark as sin, Mark and Sandeep turned off their lamps and settled back to chat about their work while I pulled a colorful wrap about myself and left my clothing behind to go for a swim in the lagoon. I'd already been swimming that day in the Vai, and we planned to swim in the lagoon the following day, but I'd never been anywhere this warm on Christmas before. So I wanted to go swimming on Christmas night, just because I could.

On an island with no lights under a starry sky with no moon, there was both mystery and adventure to going skinny dipping in the warm South Pacific Ocean. Alone under the stars, enjoying the delicious sensation of the sea all around me, I thought of my children back home and wondered what they were doing. I knew they were all gathering at my home in Maine, and I wondered if their Christmas would be white. I wondered if they were missing me as much as I missed them. I felt very close to God as I paddled in the darkness with stars so bright it seemed as if I could reach up and touch them, and I was filled with peace. God's peace. The peace of Christmas.

About the Author

Skye Taylor lives in St. Augustine, Florida, enjoying the history of America's oldest city and taking long walks along its beautiful beaches. She posts a weekly blog, volunteers with the USO, and is currently working on book four in her Tide's Way series, a time-travel romance, and a mystery novella. Her published works include: *Whatever it Takes, Falling for Zoe, Loving Meg, Trusting Will* and non-fiction essays of her experiences in the Peace Corps.

Crazy for Christmas

Karen Bostrom

The Wawa convenience store in Medford was strangely deserted as Lindsey and Dawn pulled up at the gas pump. When she'd moved out of New Jersey two years ago, this place had been mobbed, even at night. Now Lindsey's Accord was the only car at the station besides a pickup truck and an old SUV. Employees' probably. Of course, it was hours past midnight, officially Christmas Day, and several inches of new snow covered the ground and continued to drift onto old piles along the road. Most people were snug in their beds, with visions of full stockings and new electronics dancing in their heads, not driving with too little sleep and too much caffeine, struggling to stay awake.

"Dawn, we must be crazy! Normal people don't pack up a car full of presents and head north *from* Florida on this spur-of-the-moment, mother-daughter road trip to spend Christmas with relatives in Jersey! Not with the kind of horrible winter weather Aunt Clair and your cousins have already had up here!"

"Yeah, Mom. But we're not normal. We're spontaneous, remember? Positive thinkers. According to those feel-good CDs you listen to while you're driving and think I'm sleeping, we create our own experiences, so I hope this one gets better." Dawn said.

Lindsey cleared her throat. "Do you want me to remind you who came up with this plan to drive non-stop to New Jersey in December?"

"No. I know this mission was my idea, but it seemed like a great idea at the time. And we were *supposed* to get there before the snow arrived. But we're almost there, right? Safe and sound at our last stop. Me? I'm going in to manifest some hot chocolate. Want some? I'm buying." She grinned.

Lindsey shook her head. "Thanks for the pep talk, honey. Make mine coffee with lots of sugar."

"Okay." Dawn slammed the passenger door and yelled, "Meet you inside, Mom!" before dashing for the store.

Lindsey yawned as she zipped up her jacket and climbed out, feeling like she'd run a marathon. Driving for over seventeen hours today and now snow! She undid the cap on the gas tank as an attendant stepped out of the tiny booth. "Hey, lady. You're not allowed to pump your own gas, not even in a storm! I'll do it."

Lindsey handed him her credit card and smiled. She remembered one of the perks of being a Jersey Girl. The only state in the union where it's against the law to do something yourself. "Thanks. I forgot. Fill it with regular, please, and do you sell snow and ice scrapers?"

"You don't have one? In this?" The young man looked at her as if she was from outer space and then glanced at the license plate. "Oh. Florida. What are you two doing up here in the middle of the night? Governor declared a State of Emergency." He grabbed the squeegee she'd picked up and started clearing the snow and dirt from her windows for her.

"Good question! My relatives were supposed to drive

down and spend Christmas with us, but they had their own emergencies and cancelled. My daughter begged me to drive up on short notice and surprise them. Thought we'd make it there before the snow, but the traffic's been hell. And not just south of DC. Accidents, construction and delays all up and down I95. A couple wrong turns into our nation's capital and confusing GPS directions didn't help. And the scraper? I've lived in Florida too long. Forgot to check to see if it was still there. It isn't."

"That sucks," the young man said as he topped off the tank and gave her the receipt.

"Thanks for doing the windows," she said and gave him a couple dollars. "Merry Christmas! Get yourself a something hot to drink."

He nodded and shoved it into his pocket as she got into the car. "Wait a minute, ma'am. I think I got an extra ice scraper in my truck you can have. They don't sell 'em inside."

He ran off, returned with a plastic tool and passed it through the window. "Here. Merry Christmas."

Lindsey teared up. "How sweet!" she said. "Thank you so much! Let me pay you for it. It's not really an extra, is it?"

He shook his head. "Naw. But my shift is almost over and I only live five minutes from here. I'd want my mom and older sister to have an ice scraper. No big deal for me. I'll be fine. You be careful, ma'am. Take it slow. It's getting worse here but there's less snow as you go east."

She nodded and wiped her eyes. She knew Dawn thought she was corny, but she believed angels were everywhere, sometimes in unexpected forms. Even that nice young man with the tattoo and an earring. She said a silent prayer for a safe journey to Clair's house as she started the car and pulled closer to the store. This would be their last warm pit stop and cup of coffee for an hour or more. Before going in, she clicked the automatic car door locks. Habit. No one around to steal the presents on the back seat anyway she thought as she headed inside. Home stretch time.

* * * *

It'd been well over a half hour since they'd buckled their seat beats and set off on the last leg of their journey.

"Mom, driving at night is boring, but slow is even worse. You can't see much of anything at all." She pressed the "Seek" button and the radio blasted, "NJ101.5 New Jersey Fast Traffic coming up…"

"Fast traffic! What a joke!" Dawn muttered as she adjusted the volume. "No traffic at all, but we can't go fast because of closed highways, snow, and accidents!"

"At this point," Lindsey said, "I'll be satisfied with a slow trip as long as it's safe! And pleasant."

"Sorry," Dawn said, "Just a bit tired. I'll try to be less whiney." She laughed. I sound like my fifth graders, don't I?"

"You do, but that's okay. We're both way past tired. I hoped to stay on major highways. But we couldn't go on the Turnpike. It was closed. Didn't bargain on that."

"I know, Mom. But you're always telling me that things work out for the best," Dawn reminded her in her best patient teacher voice. "So this is exactly where we're supposed to be – driving this last hour or so of the trip on Route 70 right now. If not, the southern stretch of the Turnpike wouldn't have been closed and those two hotels you wanted us to stay in an hour ago would have had a vacancy, right?"

Lindsey shook her head at the irony of being turned away from shelter on this holy night. Over Dawn's objections, she'd stopped at two places, hoping to crash until morning's light, but there'd been no room at either inn. That left two-lane State Road Route 70 as their best alternative. No guiding star for them, but they'd head on.

"Well, Mom?"

Lindsey nodded. "Yes, my darling daughter. It's probably better to drive through a few inches of snow now than have to dig out of a hotel parking lot without a snow shovel after six more inches fall. So, it's *your* job to keep me awake!"

"Will do," Dawn said and changed the station. "Listen. One of your favorites!" She starting singing along with Bing Crosby. "I'm dreaming of a white Christmas."

Lindsey made a conscious effort to relax her grip on the steering wheel and breathe. "I love that song. I even love snow. It's beautiful. But I've never loved driving in it. Why Aunt Clair didn't retire to the Sunshine State, I have no clue. Normal people move out of this state, not fifty miles further down the Parkway."

"Mom, people like *you* move to Florida if their only adult child moves to Florida. Aunt Clair had no reason to leave Jersey." She laughed. "But change the subject. Look! At last! We're coming up to the first traffic circle. And there's another car on the road ahead."

Usually Lindsey dreaded approaching New Jersey's "circles" where four roads intersected and cars often merged in chaos, but this morning, it was reassuring to see another vehicle at all. She slowed to a crawl and blinked as headlights approached.

"Hey, what luck! It's got a snowplow. Maybe it's going our way. As long as I keep my distance, it'd be nice to follow someone. Let them forge through the new snow first."

She eased behind the battered truck with relief, but the driver veered south and Lindsey continued on 70 East. "Oh well, we're on our own. But there's a little less snow falling here."

"Yeah, but be careful. The radio said the closer we get to the shore, the more patches of black ice. Need a break, Mom? Want me to drive?"

"No, thanks, honey. I have more winter experience

than you. I'll let you switch at that convenience store when we turn off for Aunt Clair's place. Maybe twenty miles if I recall."

"Another hour?" Dawn asked.

"Could be. I'm fine. Why don't you close your eyes a bit? Just put the Christmas music back on before you snooze, okay?"

Dawn propped her head against a pillow and fell asleep before the next song was over. The farther she drove, the more Lindsey wished she'd started looking for a hotel sooner before all the smart travelers had filled up the rooms. She forced herself to sing along to "All I Want for Christmas is You," willing her eyes to stay fully open.

It would be so nice to reach Clair's house, surprise everyone and finally climb into bed or just crash on their couch with a nice cozy blanket. So nice. Maybe in front of the fireplace. Stockings all in a row. Hot chocolate. And say, "Good night, everyone. Merry Christmas...." So, so nice. To fall asleep. To drift off. Into sweet dreams. Oh yes....

Lindsey caught herself nodding off. *No! No! I can't fall asleep! I'm driving!* She jolted upright. *Oh, my God!* She scooted forward, sat up straighter, and gripped the steering wheel tighter.

I gotta stay awake. She cracked the window to let some frigid fresh air in and gulped the rest of her cold coffee. Even smacked her cheeks. *Maybe I should wake Dawn.* Nothing but light snow ahead, the same distance of pine trees lining each side of the way ahead. This was the worst stretch without street lights and few intersections. *Thank God I didn't veer off into the snowdrifts!*

The radio had gone fuzzy. She needed some loud music. Maybe that would wake Dawn. She looked down to hit the "seek" button for a new station for just a moment, but when she glanced back at the road, a flash of something appeared in front of her. An animal? An object blowing across?

Instinctively, she jammed on the brakes and the car started fishtailing. No traction. She eased off the pedal. Which way to steer? She struggled to remember. The direction of the skid? But which way? Left? Right?

The car spun around and around and slipped off the road, dipped to her left. The horn blasted as she lurched forward into the steering wheel and fell silent as the vehicle stopped abruptly, thrusting Lindsey back into her seat.

She closed her eyes and took a few deep breaths. She was exhausted. It would be so nice to let go. To sleep, but her heart pounded as if it would thump out of her chest. The air bag hadn't engaged. Yes, her ribs hurt a little, but no sharp pain. She glanced over at Dawn, wide-eyed and disoriented, holding her head. "Mom? What....?"

"You okay, honey? Did you bump your head?"

Dawn checked her reflection in the visor mirror. "Yeah, I kind of punched myself. There's a small cut on my nose. What happened?"

"I hit the brakes to avoid something on the road. Skidded on a patch of black ice and spun around. Looks like the pavement is on your side, not mine. I want to check outside the car before I back up or pull forward. But first I have to find my cell. It was in my lap but it must have gone flying. I need my flashlight app."

Dawn covered her cut with a small bandage she fished out of the glove box. "My cell's in my purse. Hope the reception here is okay. I'll find out where we are."

"Damn!" Lindsey muttered as she tried to pry her phone from its hiding place between the seat and the console. She finally unearthed a set of tweezers from the console and managed to grab her iPhone. "Saved! What did we ever do before having these gadgets?"

Lindsey got out and held on to the side of the car as she circled it, twisting her ankle at times on the uneven snow-covered ground. At the passenger side, she rapped on Dawn's window and said, "Tires seem okay. Hand me the snow scraper. I'll clear off the windows and reverse out of here."

Dawn found the scraper and pushed the window button but the glass didn't go down. She grabbed the handle and shoved, but the door wouldn't budge. "It doesn't work, Mom," she yelled. "I'm iced in. I'll come out your side and give you a hand."

Lindsey shook her head. "I'll come around and do it. Stay inside."

In a few minutes, she'd finished the job, slid inside, happy to be in the warm car. She took off her gloves and buckled up.

"Well, here's goes. Nice and easy." She slid the gear shifter into reverse, took off the parking brake and gently applied pressure to the accelerator. A slight movement back but then it rolled forward again. And tilted a bit more to the left.

"You're spinning the wheels, Mom," Dawn said, worried. "Want me to try it? You're tired. How about going forward?"

Lindsey counted to ten. And then twenty before responding. "I think the wheels on the driver's side are kind of stuck. Maybe if we unwrapped some of those presents and stuck the flattened boxes in back of the wheels we could get some traction? And get out of here."

That plan didn't work, but Dawn begged her mom to let her take a turn at the wheel while Lindsey pushed on the hood. For a moment, it seemed to work. Lindsey was able to push the car back a couple feet only to have it lurch off the boxes and stop, wheels spinning.

"Cut it!" Lindsey yelled and signaled the "Time out" sign. She listened as the motor shut off.

She went to the driver's side and tapped. "No, not cut the engine! I meant stop moving backward."

"Sorry," Dawn said, and turned the key in the ignition again. It kind of sputtered and groaned. She cranked it again. Just a grinding sound and silence. "I tried pumping the gas pedal. Honest."

Lindsey opened the door. "This car's fuel-injected. Don't need to pump it. Climb over to your side, honey. It just needs to rest before we try again. We do, too."

Once she got settled, she retrieved her wallet from her purse and pulled out a red, white and blue card. "Time to call for help. Thank God for AAA. Then 911 to let them know we're here." She glanced at Dawn. "Can you figure out from your phone app where we are? I can't just tell them to come find us on a deserted stretch of Route 70 in the boondocks, halfway between the 72 circle and the Manchester town line."

Dawn punched in the route to Aunt Clair's and showed Lindsey the flashing blue circle that represented their vehicle on the tiny screen. Lindsey was able to give that information to the AAA road assistance dispatcher and the local police to pinpoint their location. Both were sympathetic, but once they knew that Lindsey and Dawn were safely off the street, they told them to hunker down and wait.

It might be hours before anyone could get to them.

* * * *

"Well, we'd better turn off everything but the flashers so we don't drain the battery," Lindsey said. "But just in case someone comes along, I want them to see us and stop. I've got an idea. Do you have a marker?"

"I think so, Mom. I'm a teacher, remember? I've always got markers."

"Good. I'm going to get that reflective thing that goes on the dashboard to keep the car cool in the summer. It's in the trunk. You can write, 'Help' on it and we'll stick it on the front and side of the car under the right wiper. With a white rag or something flapping from the side mirror, if a car comes by it'll get their attention so they'll stop. I don't want them assuming this is an abandoned car."

Dawn scowled. "Who in the world would be driving by now? There's nobody around. And in this neck of the woods, would we want them to stop anyway?"

Lindsey sighed. "It's a chance I'm willing to take. And it'll make it easier for the tow truck or the police to spot us when they get here." She zipped up her coat, slipped on her gloves and got out.

In a few minutes, she'd found the sun shade and handed it to Dawn who'd gotten out of the car on the driver's side to help. "I've got the marker," Dawn said, wobbling a bit on the ice and mush. She slammed the door and walked toward the rear of the car where she unfolded the panels of the reflective screen and leaned on the snow-covered trunk to write, "HELP US!" in bold capital letters. She rounded the passenger side and walked unsteadily to where Lindsey had tied the white t-shirt. Together they propped the sign under the wiper blade and Lindsey used the battery jumper cables she'd found in the trunk to keep it stationery.

"Good thinking, Mom! You're a real scout!"

"Thanks, honey! Now let's just get back in the car. I'm freezing. And wet! We gotta get out of this weather."

Dawn made her way around the car and tried to open the driver's side. Locked. "Hurry up, Mom! Bring the keys. It's locked."

Lindsey reached into her pocket. No keys. Patted her jeans. No keys... Anywhere. Damn! "I don't have them, Dawn. I popped the trunk open before I got out. My keys are in the car. Don't you have the spare set in your coat?"

Dawn checked and started to cry. "No," she said. "I'm so stupid! I must have hit the door lock button when I got out. And my phone's on the dashboard. Do you have yours? We can call AAA. 911. Tell them we're stuck outside. They'll come sooner. Somebody's got to come help us! Maybe call Aunt Clair? Doesn't her son-in-law Matt own a garage? Maybe he could come get us."

Lindsey's shoulders' drooped. "No. I don't have my phone either. And we're not stupid. Just tired. Come back here out of the wind. We'll sit on the cardboard from those boxes, huddle together. Stay as warm as we can as we wait for help."

And pray.

* * * *

Had they dozed off? Passed out? Or died? Lindsey didn't know. No watch. No cell phone. Time seemed as frozen as her numb feet and her nose inhaling cold air through a moist scarf they were sharing. The dampness had even soaked through the waterproof fabric of her hooded jacket. Her arm had fallen asleep where Dawn had been leaning on her, trembling. She was wet and cold and miserable, her ribs still sore, but she was alive. Without her cell, she had no idea how long she'd been out of it, but she was beyond beating herself up for the situation. It was what it was.

"Let it be okay," she kept repeating silently, like a mantra for each bead in a mala or a rosary. "Thank You, God, we're safe."

Funny. It wasn't a plea. It was a knowing. *Somehow we will be okay.* Was this what people believed when they were thought they were going to die but didn't want to face it? Was she fooling herself with hallucinations and denials? She pictured Christmas dinner with Aunt Clair and all the cousins. The warm fireplace, the amazing smells, the smiling faces. The feel of padding around on hardwood floors in dry soft slippers or fuzzy socks. She and Dawn hadn't come this far to give up. They would be okay. They were in New Jersey, not the Alaskan tundra. Someone would come by. Maybe the tow truck was minutes away. Or the police.

And then she heard it. An engine approaching. Lights,

too, from the direction they'd come. "Dawn! Get up!"

Lindsey shook her daughter and rose. Her legs were stiff, but she stumbled toward the road, waving her arms at the welcome headlights. A Jeep slowly pulled up and parked on the shoulder about twenty yards away from the front of Lindsey's car. "Come on, Dawn!" she yelled. She grabbed her daughter's hand and started dragging her forward.

Two figures in Army fatigues got out and ran toward them. Soldiers. From Fort Dix? National Guard? A man and a woman.

"Need some help, ma'am?" the man said when he got to Lindsey's side.

"Oh, yes!" Lindsey said. "We had an accident and got locked out of our car without our cell phones. Don't know when the tow truck or the police will get here."

The man guided Lindsey to the Jeep. The woman took Dawn and did the same. They opened the back doors for them and helped them into the warm vehicle.

"Don't you worry. You'll be fine," the female soldier said. "I'm Angie and this is Michael. We're off duty and making our way home to share Christmas with the folks. Like you, probably. Happened to take a different way home from the base or we wouldn't have seen you."

Lindsey unwrapped her soggy scarf and peeled off her gloves. "I'm so grateful you did. Thank you so much for stopping. I'm Lindsey Ellis and this is my daughter, Dawn. We've been on the road over a day. From Florida. Thought we'd be at our destination before this snow, but one thing after another."

"No problem," Michael assured them. "We'll stay here with you till your help comes. First thing is to warm you up. How about some of Angie's hot chocolate? We've got a thermos. And I'll turn the heat up."

Lindsey and Dawn eagerly drank from the paper cups the soldier offered them. They savored the rich chocolate, and smiled as they cradled the warm cardboard in their hands. "This is heavenly! I can taste the marshmallows," Lindsey said.

"Yes, thank you so much," Dawn added. "Best hot chocolate I've ever had! No offense, Mom."

Angie laughed. "If you want, take off your wet coats and spread them out behind you to dry a bit. I can put your sneakers and socks by the vents up here. Oh, and help yourself to dry socks in that laundry basket, Lindsey."

Dawn kept her boots on, but Lindsey was thrilled to get out of her wet sneakers. How wonderful the soft dry socks felt as she slipped them on. The Jeep was so warm and cozy as she and Dawn and their two pleasant young hosts shared stories of Christmases past and plans for the future.

"This is our first Christmas home after serving in Afghanistan," Angie said as she smiled at Michael. "We spent many nights over there, dreaming of starting our own organic farm here when we returned."

"We've seen things people should never see," Michael added. "Things we both want to forget. And we're so grateful to be back home after being wounded over there. Grateful for all the little things we used to take for granted – like dry socks and graham crackers and flashlights in the dark. Singing Christmas Carols. Growing our own food. We're so glad to be here and able to share good times and do things for people – people we've loved for years and those we've just met. Folks like yourselves."

Even Dawn had dropped her usual cynicism and distrust. She allowed Michael to put some first aid cream on her nose and put a new bandage on it. She even let Angie place her hand on the bump on her forehead when Angie mentioned she was also a nurse.

Dawn closed her eyes, dozing off almost instantly.

Lindsey leaned forward. "Thank you two for helping us. We've taken up so much of your time and I'd love to repay you for your kindness. Please give me your address so I can send you something."

Angie smiled and patted her hand. "We don't need anything, Lindsey. It's been our pleasure. Just pass it on to someone else who needs help. Like you already do."

Lindsey's eyes filled up. Full of Christmas. The Jeep was like the stable and the manger of old. Not the place she'd expected to spend Christmas Eve, but it turned out to be even more special than the welcome she'd envisioned at her sister's home.

"Hey, Lindsey," Michael said. "You'd better get your jacket back on. I think your next helpers are here." He pointed to beams of white light and flashing red far ahead on the road.

"Dawn. Wake up!" Lindsey said. "Get your coat on. The police are here. We should be with our car."

They quickly bundled up, shook Michael's hand and kissed Angie on the cheek before hopping out of the Jeep.

"Thank you so much! Merry Christmas!" they both said and headed toward the police car that was now parked by their disabled vehicle.

Temporarily blinded by the headlights, flashing red lights and spotlight trained on their car, they shielded their eyes as they made their way to the driver's side.

"Are you Lindsey and Dawn Ellis?" the officer said.

Lindsey nodded.

"Sorry for the delay in getting to you and your daughter. Are you okay? We tried calling you back to give you an update, but it kept going to voicemail. Did your phone go dead?"

"No, Officer. We were trying one last time to drive out of here but ended up locked out of our car with our cells in it. Thank God, two nice soldiers stopped by and let us stay in their Jeep till you came. We were freezing."

The policeman knitted his brows. "Soldiers?" He glanced around and got out of the car with his hand on his gun. "What soldiers?"

"The ones in that Jeep over there," Lindsey pointed and swung around.

No Jeep. Dawn turned around and stared at where the Army Jeep had been parked. "They were right there," Dawn offered. "Michael and Angie. In Army fatigues. They gave us hot chocolate and graham crackers and sandwiches. They must have pulled away."

The officer paused. "I'll go check it out, ma'am." He opened the back door to his sedan and motioned for them to slide in. "Here, you ladies can wait where it's warm. I'll take a quick look at your car, too." They did as they were told and he closed the door firmly, leaving them deep in thought as they looked ahead at the place where the Jeep had been.

Dawn cleared her throat. "Mom, this is really weird. We're in the back of a police car. Caged. And we just spent a few hours in a nice warm Jeep that seems to have vanished. This officer seems to think we're nuts. And I'm wondering, too. Are we crazy?"

Lindsey took Dawn's hand in hers and shook her head. "Crazy lucky, maybe. It sure feels kind of crazy. But Dawn. Our hands are warm. Our coats are pretty dry. And I know I drank the best hot chocolate of my life and talked with some nice people for a couple hours. They probably didn't want to stop and give a statement. Just took off the other direction to get home faster."

The officer came back with a grim look on his face. He sat down behind the steering wheel and turned to face them. "Well, ladies. Your car's locked just like you said. I can see your keys and cells inside. The report shows you called the dispatcher hours ago so you've been stranded all that time in the snow. That's nerve-wracking. But it just doesn't add up."

"What doesn't?"

"The part about the soldiers helping you. I think you must be confused about when you got locked out. About the length of time. Or maybe you dreamed it."

Lindsey and Dawn looked at each other. Had he used the word "confused" to be polite or to humor them?

Lindsey finally said, "Dreamed what?"

"The Jeep, ma'am," he said. "I walked over to where you pointed and there are NO tracks there. Absolutely *no* tracks from that area going either way. Plain and simple. No tracks. Period. You must have imagined that."

Dawn shook her head, "Feel my hand, Officer. It's dry and warm. So is my coat. I tell you, we were in a different car. Call Fort Dix. They just got back from Afghanistan."

The officer scratched his head. "I think you two ladies maybe fell asleep in your car from exhaustion. Probably woke up and got locked out of your car a few minutes before I arrived. That's why you're not frozen or wet. That makes more sense."

"But, officer, we're not crazy! It really happened!" Dawn blurted out.

"Young lady, it's been a long night for me, too. I am *not* writing anything about a disappearing Jeep driven by Good Samaritan soldiers in my report when there are no tracks to prove it. No way. I'd have to take you to the hospital for psychiatric evaluation. And I'd have a lot of explaining to do, too. And paperwork. Do you want that?"

Lindsey nudged Dawn and said calmly, "Of course we don't want that, officer. You're right. We are extra tired and upset by the whole snowstorm and accident. We just want to get our car towed, get to my sister's house and enjoy Christmas together. Just like you and your family, right?"

He nodded. "Exactly. And look. Here's your real Christmas miracle. Looks like a tow truck coming. A major holiday in the boondocks and your tow truck shows up before daybreak. You ladies really are lucky on a night like this!"

"Yes, we are, Sir. Very lucky." Lindsey squeezed

Dawn's hand and whispered, "And blessed."

"Good. I'll finish up my report. Come back and sign it before you go. I need to chat with the driver. If he can get your car out of here, I'll have to tag it and make a notation of that, too," he added.

The driver was able to unlock their vehicle and get the keys, but it wouldn't start. "Battery seems okay but it sounds like you might need a starter, ma'am," he said. "Get what you need out of the car before I put it on the flatbed. I'll tow you up to one hundred miles...but I'd prefer closer."

"Me, too," Lindsey agreed, relieved that she didn't have to drive any further. "Don't worry. I know it's much closer than that. I'll get my things out of the car and touch base with the policeman first. Be right back." Along with some personal items, she grabbed one of the tins of Christmas cookies intended for their relatives and headed to the police car.

After she updated the patrolman about being towed, she handed him the gift and added, "Thank you so much for coming to our rescue, Officer. Merry Christmas!"

He grinned and opened the tin. "Chocolate chip. My favorite. Thanks, Ms. Ellis. It's been...an *interesting* experience." He winked and handed her a clipboard. "I left out the part about the Jeep. And FYI, the tow truck driver came from the other direction, and he swore he didn't see any Jeep pass him either. No other tracks. Just sayin'... You might want to leave that soldier part out, too, when you tell your story. Sounds more... normal."

Lindsey skimmed and signed his report. As he'd promised, he stayed until the tow truck got their car out of the snowdrift and onto the flatbed. Lindsey and Dawn climbed into the seat of the truck and sang Christmas Carols with the driver, all three of them glad that Matt's garage was less than fifteen miles away and that the snow had stopped.

It was daybreak when Dawn called her cousin Bonnie

who was already up with her husband Matt and their eager children, emptying stockings and opening gifts. He promised to meet them at his garage and was sworn to secrecy about them being in New Jersey until they were able to surprise Clair in person later.

At the garage, after they gave the driver a big tip and transferred all their packages and suitcases to Matt's SUV, Dawn whispered to Lindsey, "Things really do work out for the best, don't they, Mom? Even if it doesn't feel so good at times."

Lindsey nodded. "Yes, they do, honey. And this idea of yours to surprise Aunt Clair at Christmas? A truly inspired idea!"

* * * *

Later, as they sat side by side drinking mugs of hot chocolate by Aunt Clair's fireplace, Dawn leaned over to Lindsey and said, "Mom, at dinner, when you were telling everybody about our accident coming here, you left out the part about the policeman not seeing the Jeep tracks in the snow. We're not really crazy, are we? It really did happen, didn't it?"

Lindsey hesitated. "What do you think, honey?"

"Well, I think we may be crazy in our own way. But the whole Jeep thing really happened. I know it did! Even if it's not logical." She paused a moment, before whispering, "It gives me goose bumps, but I kind of think they were angels. Real angels. Here they were, total strangers, and I felt totally comfortable and cared for. Is that weird?"

Aunt Clair interrupted them. "Angels? Did you meet some angels on your trip here?" she asked with a wink.

Lindsey reached over to hug her. She smiled and pointed to the green Army socks on her feet. "We did, I guess. They cared for us while we were locked out of the car, but when the police and tow truck came, it seemed our rescuers had never been there. But I'm wearing the socks that Angie gave me."

"Don't ever let anyone talk you out of believing in the angels, girls. They are all around us, for sure," Aunt Clair said softly. "Just be grateful."

"Oh, I am," Lindsey said with a smile. "All the lovely people who acted like angels on our way – from the young man with the ice scraper to the officer who didn't insist on taking us to the hospital to check our sanity. And, of course, I'm grateful for my sometimes angelic but always amazing and adventurous daughter!"

Dawn smiled. "Thanks, Mom! I'm grateful for you, too! Merry *White* Christmas!"

"Hear, hear," crowed Aunt Clair with her hot cocoa raised high in the air.

"Thank you! But next year, I'm going to insist on a *warm* Christmas on a sandy beach!"

About the Author

Karen Bostrom is the author of DANGEROUS SANDS, a contemporary romantic suspense novel set at the Jersey Shore. She's also published in several short story collections. A retired elementary school technology teacher, she's an accomplished ballroom dancer, a Reiki healer-in-training, an artist and a world traveler.

My Prayer Buddy

Sharon E. Buck

It had been a rough week. Injured in a serious car accident, I was 48, recuperating at my parents' home, and having a pity party for one.

Glancing across the room, I saw my prayer buddy sitting on the nightstand. A warm sense of peace and love gently enveloped me; "My peace I give to you, my peace I leave with you," whispered tenderly in my mind.

I smiled as I flashed back to the previous Christmas. I was living in Birmingham, Alabama, broke, in debt, renting a room from a nice, older lady, trying desperately to keep my one-person company afloat. My vehicle hiccupped and burped around town, and depression nipped at my heels day and night. Not wanting to spend Christmas alone, something I had done countless times over the years, I called my sister in Covington, Tennessee.

Would it be all right if I came to spend Christmas with her and her family? Hearing the warmth of yes from a loved one, I felt relieved and welcomed. The doom and gloom evaporated as surely as if I had stepped in a shower and washed away layers of dirt.

Her new home was huge, filled with three children, a husband, two cats, and a hyperactive, perpetual motion thing they called a dog, (he demonstrated normal behavior for a Jack Russell terrier, I later found out). An unbelievable sense of love permeating the house, like the fragrance of fresh baked sugar cookies.

While catching up on life with my sister, I noticed my one of my twelve-year-old twin nieces sitting at the kitchen table carefully taking little pieces of various colored clay and pressing them together A small form appeared. Meticulously, she created what appeared to a shepherd boy.

"What's that, Christina?"

She looked up at me with big, dark brown puppy dog eyes, and a slight smile. "It's a prayer buddy, Aunt Sharon." Turning her attention back to the clay person, she added, "It's for a friend."

Watching her press the flesh color clay on top of blue sleeves, creating hands in a prayer clasp, I remembered thinking, 'she really loves whoever she's making that for.'

Later that day I was in the kitchen with my sister, and noticed bits and pieces of broken clay on the countertop. The only thing apparently able to withstand the heat of the oven was Christina's prayer buddy.

There he sat on his knees patiently, hands together in prayer, and his coal black eyes focused in a knowing stare, seeing that he was *in* this world but not *of* this world. Love radiated from the beautiful piece of baked clay. I wanted one.

"Christina, will you make me one before I leave?" I asked her.

"Um, sure." A non-committal answer.

Christmas morning was a wonderful celebration of love, with handmade gifts. Children's fingers anxiously ripped through carefully wrapped Christmas paper.

Squeals of delight came from the twins and their ten-year-old sister with each gift unwrapped.

My gifts were wrapped with love by inexperienced fingers that struggled to fold uncooperative paper and put tape on the packages. I couldn't have loved them any more than if they had come from the most expensive store on Rodeo Drive.

Opening Christina's package gently, I just stared at her gift in total surprise.

"I was going to give him to you anyway," she said shyly.

There he was! The little shepherd, kneeling, dressed in a blue robe, white head cloth with a gold band, dark hair peeking out, black eyes, and hands clasped in prayer.

"He's your prayer buddy, so you'll always have someone to pray with and you'll never be alone," she explained with a smile and shining eyes.

It was all I could do to keep from sobbing like a fool. To receive a gift made from loving hands; a gift presented from the heart; a gift that no money could ever purchase; the gift of one's self; a gift so pure that my heart ached with something I had no words to describe.

The gift of love was so great that I realized, in a small way, of what God's love must be for each one of His children. The gift embodied everything and more that I could ever hope to have in my life: A gentle, beautiful reminder of what God offers to each one of us.

Looking at the prayer buddy now, and the times I had picked it up during the course of the year, I felt the love come through. A love that declared firmly many, many times, 'where two or more are gathered in His name'.

Praying for whatever it was at that time, I realized how something as simple as a *prayer buddy* always reminded me of God's love and how He was always present for us.

The most precious gift I received that year was a

prayer buddy—and a reminder that God is always there for *me*.

About the Author

Sharon E. Buck is a professional writer with a wickedly delightful sense of humor. Author of *A Dose of Nice*, a Southern Chick Lit humorous murder mystery, and five other less funny books – okay, they're how-to books, but whatever, Sharon is currently at work on *A Honky Tonk Night* and *Being a Parent to Parents*. "Everything's funny with aging parents...just not while you're living it in the moment." Contact Sharon via her website www.SharonEBuck.com.

Faith, Hope and Tyler

Dianne Nerad Ell

This story is dedicated to Dr. Eric Searcy, Dr. John Yselonia and the staff at Antigua Veterinary Practice, St. Augustine, Florida. May they always have a blessed and happy Christmas.

There are two means of refuge from the miseries of life: music and cats. – Albert Schweitzer

Much has been written about cats. They've appeared as heroes and villains in plays, books, television programs, movies, articles of various kinds and just recently there were the results of a study that showed just how smart cats are. But this isn't so much a tale about a cat as it is about the veterinarian who saved him.

The journey to find a new furry family member began in May of that year. Nine months before, our beloved Caesar had gone over the rainbow and after twenty years of living with a most phenomenal cat, we hesitated to bring another into our family. But the time had come. There was just me and my husband and we needed to open our lives and hearts to a cat in need of love and a home.

The search began with the adoption centers of local pet stores. From there we migrated to the animal shelters both north and south of where we lived in northeast Florida. But with all of our searching we didn't make a connection. The timing wasn't right.

We waited. Summer passed. As did autumn. Then in late November we decided to give it another try. It was nearing Christmas. Maybe the timing was better. The weather had gone from the heat of early summer to the chill of a late fall. On the day we started out, a rain dampened the landscape but not our spirits. We took the path we did before, but by the time we headed toward the animal shelter in the county to the south of us, we were getting discouraged. The shelter was a forty-five minute ride south over a flat, open fields bordered by pines and oaks and was soggy with rain. During the drive we talked about what we were looking for in our future family member. We wanted a breed different than Caesar who had been a golden tabby, and we were hoping for an older cat. Maybe female.

The animal shelter was built on several acres of land and had many rooms devoted to cats, dogs, and other animals. We walked down aisles and looked through the glass into rooms where the cats lived. If we saw one with whom we made visual contact, we went to the room where they could meet us, and us, them. The interview room had different toys and devices where both parties could meet and decide if there's a match. We 'talked' to about a half dozen cats but it wasn't working out. They were all so adorable. They were all so much in need. But the connection needed to be the right one and it wasn't.

We decided that today was not the day, but as we headed down the hall toward the reception area, we passed by a room where several cats were jumping around and playing. In the midst of the chaos was a brown kitten, sound asleep on a mat.

Even though he didn't know we were looking at him, we both immediately felt something. We asked to see him and they brought him back to the interview room. He was a small, brown tabby. He was still half asleep but the moment he saw us his eyes lit up. He reached out for me. I held him then handed him over to my husband. They played together for a few minutes and that was all it took. We were both in love.

We brought the kitten home. It was the Thursday before Thanksgiving. Our kitten was happy. He knew he was home. He played with the toys we had ready for him, and that night showered us with lots of kitty kisses. He was an adorable cat. We knew we would be his forever family. We named him Tyler.

The next morning, Friday, we noticed that his left eye was weeping. Since we wanted to get him to the vet for an overall checkup, I called the one the shelter recommended, and we were able to get in that afternoon. The checkup revealed Tyler had lots of problems, the kind that animals get in shelters, but nothing serious. We brought him home with medication and thought all was well with our beloved new family member. Then the next day, the diarrhea started. We didn't understand why. He was eating the dry and wet food that we got from the vet. But the problem continued. On Monday we returned to the old Victorian house that housed the animal clinic. And thus began a journey that would never be forgotten.

The vet, a very experienced doctor with many years of treating all types of diseases, examined Tyler then asked that we leave Tyler with him. He needed to do more tests and being there overnight was the only way he could monitor Tyler's progress. We agreed. We went home and then came back bringing Tyler his new blue and white blanket and some toy mice to keep him company.

Thanksgiving came and went but Tyler remained at

the animal hospital. At the end of the week, we brought him home. But within a few hours we knew that he still had his problem. It not only continued it seemed worse. It was distressing to us, but it was particularly upsetting to Tyler. He'd move away from where he just 'went' and stare at it. He'd look up at us, then back down at the mess. He was small and pathetic looking. He almost looked like he was crying. We felt so bad for him.

Again, we called the vet and back Tyler went. It was early December. For the next two weeks Tyler was at the animal hospital more than home. Tests were done over and over, but he wasn't responding to treatment. And again we brought Tyler home for the weekend.

On Monday, the vet called us in. The results of all the tests were back and the news was as bad as it could possibly be. It didn't look as though Tyler would recover. Whatever he had picked up either in the shelter or his days of living in a gas station parking lot was deep in his system.

The last step would be to put Tyler to sleep, but before that, the vet asked us if we would give him and Tyler one more chance. The vet still had one more trick up his sleeve. He asked for one more week with Tyler. It was December 17th. We gladly gave it to him. That night, we visited Tyler. He was sad, listless, and looked ready to give up. We sat him on the counter in the visiting area and his 'daddy' told him that we were not giving up on him. We were with him no matter what it took. And he was not to give up on himself. He seemed to understand and his eyes brightened.

On Monday, December 24th, the vet called and said he had done all that was humanly possible for Tyler. We picked up our little ball of fur and returned home with him. There wasn't any way we would put Tyler to sleep if at possible. He was member of our family. We loved him and as long we could make him comfortable, he would live out his life with us.

Monday night, Christmas Eve, the diarrhea was still there but not as bad. He had climbed into his box to go but hadn't quite made it. I assured him it was okay. I petted his head then he leaned against me and I held him.

Christmas morning, I crept into the sitting room where we kept Tyler's litter box. I looked in knowing what I'd see ... but I didn't.

I stared. I sifted through the granules of litter but didn't see anything except remnants of urine. I couldn't believe it. I wasn't ready yet to tell my husband, but Tyler understood. He came up to the box and looked in. Then went through the cat door to the porch. All day throughout dinner, opening presents, watching a Christmas movie, I kept going back to the potty box or just looked around to see if Tyler's health issue was visible. It wasn't.

Christmas night, after dinner, Tyler indicated that he wanted me to see something. This adorable little ball of brown striped fur with short legs led me to the back of the house and the sitting room where his litter box was kept. And there, as he looked proudly down at it, was the first normal bowel movement Tyler had since we brought him home from the shelter. It was an incredible, joyful time for a little cat who had suffered so much. I knew he was happy. I cried as I picked him up, hugged him, then we went in search of his 'daddy' so he could share in Tyler's excitement. Now I had hope that Tyler would actually recover.

We waited a few days before calling the vet and letting him know his magic had worked. It appeared Tyler was cured. Wherever the vet's knowledge led him, it was to a medication that killed the parasite and would allow Tyler to live and return to a normal life.

We have now celebrated our second Christmas with Tyler. Exceptional times call for exceptional measures. The veterinarian, Dr. Searcy, who treated Tyler, who did not give up on him, or on his own amazing skills, needs to be remembered. He will be a part of our lives as much as our now slightly more grown up cat is.

Tyler has proven to be unique in his own way. As he's grown, his fur has become thick like a bear's. He sometimes stands on his hind legs like a grizzly bear. He watches over the ducks on the lake behind us letting us know when it's time to feed them. He takes seriously his job of watching the house while we're gone and he gets the greatest joy out of talking to and playing with his small stuffed mice. He still has his baby face and hopefully always will out of which the most beautiful turquoise eyes gaze upon the world.

Life doesn't always turn out in the way we'd like it to. In fact, most of the times it doesn't. It takes us down other paths which end up in greater disasters or brings us to a road we wouldn't have found otherwise. Our search for another cat was meant to be the way it turned out. Without us, without the help of a very special, amazing vet, Tyler on his own, wouldn't have made it to Christmas.

But on the December 24th, when he left the animal clinic, he left without having to return for further treatment or medication. He is strong. He is healthy. He chases anything that moves and is prone, in his desire to say 'thank you', to bring us everything from lizards to dragonflies.

In the end we didn't end up with a different breed or a female, older cat. We ended up with Tyler. A male, brown striped Tabby kitten.

In the end, you go where your heart and destiny take you.

About the Author

Dianne Neral Ell has written for trade and consumer publications, online magazines and websites. Her previous suspense novel, *The Exhibit* was a TOR/Forge publication. Her short story, "Last Man Standing" was published by *Sherlock Holmes Mystery Magazine* in 2015. She is a member of the Mystery Writers of America, Author's Guild and Florida Writers Association.

The Old Man and the Zinneas

Christine W. Kulikowski

Someone knocked on his door. He didn't answer.

They knocked harder. He didn't answer. The knob turned slowly and the door opened a crack.

"Tomasz? Tomasz, can I come in?"

It was Sister Anna's voice. Funny—his wife was called Anna; she died of a heart attack twenty years ago. *She wasn't a bad wife.* He'd made sure she and the kids had everything they needed. *Not a bad marriage, as marriages go.*

"Tomasz! Tomasz! Are you okay? Can I come in?"

"Tak," he grunted. *Yes.*

Sister Anna's parents were Kowalski's from Tarnow in Poland, his home of the heart. Her job was to harass inmates in this Florida hellhole.

"Tomasz, it's noon and you haven't opened the shades," Sister said, fluttering her hands at the covered windows.

"There's nothing to see." The sun reflecting from all the white coral on the paths and parking lots seared his eyes. *She doesn't speak Polish. Shame on her parents.*

His kids could yell at him in perfect Polish.

"You haven't had your breakfast. Why don't you come to the cafeteria for lunch? It's *bigos* today."

He liked that mix of sauerkraut and pork. Besides, she would blather at him until he followed. One time when he wasn't hungry for a couple of days she called a brain doctor who wanted to push pills on him. Depression was the diagnosis. Tomasz had asked him if *he* wouldn't be depressed when strangers put him in prison in an unknown country and gave orders all day. Doc got the point and left. Later, Sister Anna asked the old man if he knew where he was. *In Florida, good old USA, locked up with crazies in "assisted living."* What a stupid question.

He sat at an empty table in the cafeteria. Well, it wasn't a cafeteria. They prettied it up with tablecloths. *Plastic.* Plastic flowers, too. *Cheap ones.* No fake zinnias, though. His favorite flower. He should be working in his garden in New Jersey; he had to get ready for sowing zinnias. He shook his head angrily. There would *never* be zinnias again.

In the mess hall he couldn't choose what he wanted. *Like in prison.* One of those ugly green blackboards hung on the wall. It always said, "Today's Special." Nothing un-special to order. He knew the menu by heart: bigos on Monday, spaghetti on Tuesday . . .he didn't think noodles were a meal. *Some cafeteria.*

A woman in a pastel pink uniform brought him bigos and coffee. She was too old to wear baby pink. He needed vodka, not coffee. Anger burned in his eyes briefly and cut off his breathing. He gagged on the anger. *Damned kids.*

Before he could finish a cough, he was surrounded. One huge guy in white jumped him and squeezed his arms around his belly and tried to choke him. Sister Anna took his blood pressure. There was a cart of medical stuff behind her.

"What are you doing? Let go of me."

"Are you able to breathe now, Tomasz? Take your time. You're safe now."

"I was safe before. Can't a man clear his throat?" This time he roared. He wanted them to hear him. "I need protection from *you*. Get me back to New Jersey before you kill me. Is that enough breathing for you?"

They didn't apologize. Sister Anna smiled sweetly at him. That's all she *ever* did. Probably thought how great they were saving an old guy. They'd be old someday, if they were lucky. And they would be locked up like him.

Kids. He had six of them. They'd deported him to this place of old men and older women. Sure he was old; why couldn't they leave him alone? His two-family house in Paterson was *his* house.

Paterson . . . Lou Costello came from there. Did anyone remember Lou Costello? Great comic. The old man knew his house needed lots of work. He was getting everything in shape. No hurry. They tried to hire plumbers, electricians, roofers and he wouldn't stand for it. He *never* let anyone touch his property. *It was my house.* He worked eighty hours a week in a stinking textile mill to buy that home. *Mine. Only mine.* He was eighty and strong like a bull, just like his father.

That meddling neighbor shouldn't have called the kids. So he fell off the ladder, but not from high up. He was nowhere near the roof. He knew what cracked ribs felt like. Some rubbing alcohol and a scarf tied hard against his chest were all he needed. Instead all six landed on him, dragged him to a doctor who took x-rays. The Doc decided that he should tie a binder around his chest and take pain killers. He'd refused, of course. The Doc said the scarf was good enough. A little aspirin and vodka killed pain better than any fancy pill, but he didn't ask the Doc about that. He was glad to see his kids' embarrassment. *I was right, not them.*

They still wouldn't let him alone. They said the house

was dangerous because all his things were stuffed in every room. So what? They weren't anybody else's. *My things. My rooms.*

He needed *everything.* He might need the exact nail they wanted to throw out. Then they asked the gossiping neighbor to cook for him. She made disgusting messes of "nutrition." No salt. No butter. No sugar in the coffee.

But the end was when she said she would help organize his things. He knew where *all* his things were. It was no business of hers if he liked his clean shirts on top of his good hammer and chisel. He'd kicked the woman out but not before he told her to organize herself. He was tempted to use coarse language, but didn't. She would whine to the kids and they would come running.

He was deaf, but not as deaf as *they* were. They didn't hear one word he'd said. They stopped trying to help him. *But I didn't know they were planning to betray me.*

An old lady in pastel blue hair was at his table telling him the cafeteria was closing. Blue hair! At least it wasn't pink. He got up and left. He hadn't eaten. He wasn't hungry. And he wasn't doing women's work by taking his dishes to the kitchen. The nuns were in the business of helping old geezers like him. Let them have the pleasure.

Sister Anna ambushed him outside his room.

"You didn't eat your bigos. What happened?"

What happened? She and two thugs tried to kill him. He shook his head and walked around Sister Anna. She wouldn't let up. Who was the tattle-tale that told her he didn't eat? *Spies everywhere.*

"Tomasz, you know it's less than three weeks to Christmas, don't you?"

He didn't know or care.

"Some friends are practicing Polish carols. We should go have a look."

Some nerve. "We" should this, "we" shouldn't that.

I'm not a "we." He was an "I." He didn't have friends here. Most of his real ones were dead and buried. He turned his back on her and went into his room.

"You go. I won't," he muttered.

Sister Anna smiled that damn holy smile.

"I don't sing," he grumbled.

"Have a rest, Tomasz. I'll come by later."

Of course she would. She clung to him like a bur. No one else tried talking to him except her. In three months, he'd insulted everybody except Sister Anna. Being alone wasn't a bad thing. His father hadn't been called "Wilk," The Wolf, for nothing. He'd been a lone wolf all his life. He lived to 95, through the Russian Revolution, two World wars, Communist occupation, and Marshall Law without a murmur. He was tough and had made his son tough.

When a horse kicked twelve-year-old Tomasz and tore open his foot down to the bone, his father didn't panic. He gave Tomasz a cup of vodka and used that same magic potion to wash the wound; then he stitched it with a darning needle and button thread. The witch next door—they call them herbalists now—mixed some secret ingredients and poured them on a plant called "God's Gift." It had large fuzzy leaves. She packed his foot with the leaves, tied everything with a woolen scarf, and said she would have another look in two months.

He was fine by then and out plowing with the same horse that had kicked him. They only had one. He had eleven brothers and sisters, not counting the ones who died. He adored his father but the others didn't. He still missed him *and* that horse.

"Tomasz? Why aren't you going into your room? Are you all right?"

Did she have a camera in his room? Or was this part of the plan to drive him crazy?

"Okay, okay. Yes. I am. Can't a man think?" He went inside, locked his door and laid down on his battered old sofa from home. They'd tried to throw it out, those ungrateful children.

"Get a nice new one, Tata. Please, Daddy. You'll feel better." How did they know what I would feel? Or feel right now. They wanted him to say he was happy so they could feel they'd done their duty.

His sofa knew him better than the kids did. It cradled his aching knees and feet. It splinted his head just right. He could lie on his side to watch TV. His neck and back didn't hurt too bad. The sofa understood his needs better than his wife had.

"Tomasz? Tomasz? I have something for you," that sweet, tormenting voice called through the closed door.

He groaned. He hated the motions of sitting up, getting his feet on the floor, and then standing up. But, he had to—he'd locked his door. *No telling what she'll do if I don't open the door...*

The nun never stopped bothering him. He opened the door and there she stood, holding a tray of drinks. No alcohol, he knew.

"I'll leave these for you. We musn't get dehydrated. You will like one of them."

He wouldn't. No point arguing. He was tired. Would he go to hell or purgatory if he killed this nun?

"Put them on the table. Thank you. Good bye."

She disappeared quickly. No more talk. He left his door unlocked and laid down again.

They wanted him to sit in an armchair. Better for his circulation. There was nothing wrong with his circulation. The seat was hard on his rear end; the chair was too small so his elbows went numb leaning on the arms. It was not his. It didn't know him. Anger flushed over his face again. *They threw out my perfectly good armchair.* Sure it smelled. All his dogs liked to sit with him. And if it stunk it was nobody's business. He didn't mind.

The old man thought his kids would leave him alone after he kicked out that neighbor. They tricked him, though; they got papers from a lawyer to say he was nuts and put him in a home for old crazy people. In Florida. St. Petersburg. In a Polish asylum. *They call it assisted living. Huh.*

He had a big TV from the kids. He liked watching sports and cowboy films but it wasn't enough to make a life. In Paterson he had a garden. He planted a whole meadow of zinnias every year. Sometimes he added cosmos, but it was zinnias he loved. Small men speaking Spanish did the gardening here. He didn't speak Spanish and they didn't speak Polish or English. He wanted to tell them their plants were ugly: all spines, thorns, and strange colors. Native species, Sister Anna had told him. He missed zinnias.

His back ached. A swallow of vodka would help. But the keepers said old people couldn't drink alcohol. It interfered with their pills. He didn't take pills. They didn't answer. But he got no vodka.

The phone rang. It was a real phone. Large. Black. With a dial. Those cell phones weren't any good. Tiny buttons. His gnarled fingers couldn't hit them right. He decided to answer it. He had to. The kids would call Sister Anna to check on him.

"Tata?"

It was his daughter, Krysia. He couldn't be angry at his favorite child. His only girl. *She didn't side with the boys. She cried for me.* She was so smart, so sweet. She was a Professor of Rocks; he didn't know why rocks needed studying at Rutgers University. But everyone respects a Professor. He was proud of her.

She was the only one to give him a grandchild. Alicia was three. She was his joy. A blessing in his old age. And, he probably would never see her again. The thought almost made him choke. *No choking!* He cleared his throat and listened to her sweet voice.

"How are you, Tata? Sister Anna says you won't eat and just stay in your room." *Women. Gossipers.*

"The food isn't too good. I'm not allowed to do anything for exercise. They want me to play shuffleboard." *Sissies pushing a hockey puck.* He didn't push things unless he was working. "I watch a hockey game if I want to see a puck bouncing all over the place." *Give me a wheelbarrow full of cement for repairs, that's exercise. No sidewalks here anyway. Just antsy-pantsy white paths.*

"Krysia, are you there?" *Maybe she hung up.*

"Yes, Tata, I was listening very carefully. Is there *anything* you like? It's a place for Polish people to retire. I thought you would like being around Poles like you."

He wanted to explode, but didn't.

"These people aren't like me. No one from Tarnow. They play checkers and gossip all day. The men, too. I never went to the Polish Falcons Lodge in Paterson for good reason. Bunch of drunken idiots. I tried talking to these inmates about the war, or about Pilsudski and Sikorski. They don't even know who they were."

"Tata, we will all visit you for Christmas. Alicia, too. I have an idea for your present. The boys will be calling you. Please don't yell at them. They'll stop calling."

"Let them. They put me here." *They didn't listen before, they don't listen now. Who cares if they don't call?*

"Tata, here's Alicia. She wants to tell you she loves you." The little voice told him she loved him. In Polish. Krysia knew how to raise a Polish child. He felt a warmth inside and allowed himself a smile.

"Good bye, Tata. We'll see you soon," his daughter said softly.

He laid down the receiver. And then stretched out on his sofa and cried. He was *so* lonely. Better not show it, though, or Sister Anna would drag him to some other "social event." He wouldn't waste time on *this* society. TV was better.

*****

The boys called. One every day. They probably put him on their *schedules*. Despite his words to Krysia, the old man waited for those calls. They were water to a thirsty man.

Casimir was the head lawyer at some famous company. He was like his mother; she could turn black into white. Marcin had his own company making expensive furniture by hand. His furniture was in museums.

Jakub wrote books. Difficult books about history and wars. He was even on TV sometimes. Michal was an actor. He didn't act in foolish plays. He went to London for Shakespeare and Balzac. Little Tomaszek was named after him. He was the youngest and the strangest. He painted. Mostly flowers and plants. Somehow he made a living. He sold cards with his paintings on them. And prints. He sold some paintings big as a table to a bank and a hotel.

The old man wept after every phone call. He loved them *all* so much. He wasn't sure about them. They had lives away from his. Why didn't they want him around?

They couldn't stand him anymore; he was just in the way.

*****

The old man ate less and less. He moved around less. He stopped watching TV. He stopped answering phone calls. He refused to wash. The psychiatrist came again. He talked to the old man. The old man glared at him but wouldn't talk. He offered pills again. The old man refused again. The psychiatrist spoke to Sister Anna in the hallway.

"He still gets furious. That's good." They walked away whispering to each other. Two days later Sister Anna walked in.

"It's Christmas Eve. Get up! We have the Vigil tonight. Your kids are all coming to the Vigil and your granddaughter, too. You don't want Alicia to see her Dziadzia looking like a homeless person, do you? Her Grandpa is her hero."

The old man sat up. His eyes lost their absent look. *Alicia.*

"I *am* a homeless person. But let's get it over with." He didn't want to let Sister Anna see how joyful he was. He went to the shower telling Sister Anna to get out of the shower room. He still had his modesty. He felt much better all cleaned up and shaved. He stepped onto the floor and picked up the towel and robe Sister Anna left him. He opened the door. Outside waiting for him was one of those young men who had attacked him. Well, this time he was ready.

"Don't touch me. I know where my cage is."

He wanted the youngster to know he didn't need anyone to help him. In his room he picked out a shirt from the new clothes they had left him. A red-checked shirt was just right for Alicia. Khaki work pants made him feel like a man again. So did his shiny black shoes. The young man lurking outside knocked to see if he was ready.

Of course, he was. *Alicia.* He settled in his uncomfortable chair and waited. He remembered to tune in a cowboy show. Bonanza. His kids shouldn't think he was lonely without them. *Even if I am.*

He was nodding off when the door burst open. No knocking.

"Dziadziu, Dziadziu, please come home I love you I made my handprint for you." She paused to catch her breath. "And lots of pictures."

She smelled like sunshine as she climbed on his lap.

"She draws lots and lots of pictures, Tata. Their weight could crash a plane, so we brought just fifty of her favorites." Krysia smiled. A smile sweeter than Sister Anna's.

"Where's that lazy bunch of bums?" he snarled

though a smile tugged at his lips despite his attempts to contain it.

Krysia laughed. As though on cue, the grown men who once were his babies rushed in and surrounded his chair. They hugged and kissed him almost to suffocation.

Maybe they love me after all.

They all chattered at once about their work, their accomplishments, and their loneliness with him so far away. They thanked him for the eighty hours he labored in searing heat and a miasma of chemicals to educate them. They remembered.

Sister Anna peeked in, smiling broadly. "Come to the rec room for Vigil and songs."

The old man didn't hesitate. Getting to his feet, he took Alicia's hand. She skipped down the hall, but not before she glanced around to see where her mother was.

"I'm not supposed to tell you," she whispered loudly as only little girls do. "We have a huge present for you. Bigger than this place. Bigger than the sky." Her childish Polish had his heart skipping beats.

The rec room sparkled with lights and tinsel. Three trees stood in the corners: one in blue, one in traditional multi-colors, and one with handmade ornaments from the residents and local schoolchildren. The old man thought the place looked okay. The white tablecloths were real. A little hay peeked out from under each like hay from Jesus' manger.

Alicia was delighted. With a glance up at him and a grin, she joined the other children running around, touching the decorations, and squealing excitedly. The old man sat at a long table with all his family. He stopped visitors and residents to introduce them and boast of their achievements. His "neighbors" seemed startled by his merriment. *Now, I'm a happy man.*

The children crowded around the windows as they waited for the first star. They laughed their way through the Vigil fish dinner. Everyone exchanged white wafers pressed with biblical Christmas themes. Everyone sang carols. The old man sang along loudly.

At midnight the visiting priest celebrated Mass. Most youngsters were asleep but not Alicia. The old man was proud. She was tough, like him. When Mass was over the sleepyheads woke as one and rushed to the tree for presents.

They ate candies, dried fruit, and poppy cake. Then the families wished one another *Wesolych Swiat*, Happy Holydays, and each headed for their own rooms to open presents and talk till morning.

Family crowded the old man's room. They sat on the sofa, the chair and the bed. They all looked at the old man expectantly. Alicia was the host. She introduced her mother.

"Mama is Saint Nicholas. She will tell the story of the big present for Dziadziu. There are no presents for the uncles. But I have pictures for them."

The old man chuckled. His little darling was as sharp as a needle.

"Tata," his daughter said, "we are unhappy because you are unhappy. You said you wanted to live in a Polish nursing home to talk to old men who knew the truth about the war and the evil Russians."

Had he said that? He didn't remember. Why didn't they remember the good stories? They remembered the stupid stuff.

"Sister Anna called us every week. She told us how angry, aggressive, and lonely you were—don't argue, you were angry and aggressive. We had to plan something better for you."

The old man looked at his sons. Were they part of a new scheme? *Now what? Could anything be worse?* His body tensed. He felt his smile vanish. Where would they send him next? *Poland.* He hated the new Poland. Alicia ran to his lap.

"Be happy." She curved his lips into a smile. "You will love, love, love your present. It's not wrapped. Too, too big."

"Dad—oops—Tata," Marcin, the furniture maker said, "we decided we had to be closer to you."

A nursing home in New Jersey?

"Dad," Casimir said without correction, "you will have to sign an agreement as to what you must do and what not."

The old man never knew what Casimir meant when he talked like the big time lawyer. He sighed. Then he looked around for an interpreter.

Jakub, the serious writer, spoke up. "Cas, what are you doing? Already with signing forms? Tata, we took over your house."

The old man blanched. He tightened his hold on Alicia who sat very still.

"To renovate and upgrade—just let me finish."

The old man shut his mouth. *They fixed my house. They're selling my house. My house—mine—my house.* He couldn't breathe. He was suffocating again.

"Tata, what's wrong? Get some water, Cas. Daddy, breathe. You will live in your house again," she gushed as though her words could bring him life. "It's yours. Forever."

He whooshed out the air stuck in his lungs. He took a fresh breath. His mind couldn't absorb Krysia's words.

"You didn't sell it already? For the money?" he gasped.

Krysia laughed. Laughing? At what was she laughing?

"We couldn't sell your house. The city wanted to condemn it. So we demolished it to the frame and started fresh. It's beautiful."

"Taxes. More taxes. No money." Could he believe this? He could leave this purgatory? Dollars. He would manage. He still could get a job.

"Father," Cas said, "I filled out the legal paperwork. Krysia will manage the taxes and house maintenance."

The old man gurgled a laugh. His Kazio was born for law. When he was three, he wrote a contract for Jakub. Which books would go on which book case. Jakub carried off books but never returned them.

"Mama, tell him now," Alicia mumbled, almost asleep.

"Tata, I'm moving in on the second and third floors. You can see Alicia every day. I put a freezer in your kitchen for good old Polish meals."

He shrugged. "I can fix things when they break. I can repair the roof."

His sons moaned in unison. Krysia gave them That Look.

"No, Tata. There's nothing to repair. But before taking you home, I need some promises. A contract. You must sign. You won't try to repair or improve the house. I have good contractors on call. You can cook a little. We put an oversize TV in the living room—cable."

"I like TV, but I need work."

"I know. The garage is now a workshop."

"I've got to fix the doors."

"They're fixed. It's a fine room now. Shelves, workbenches, a small TV, and a coffee maker. All those great windows are new."

"It's too hot."

The boys were making good-bye noises. Again Krysia gave them That Look. They settled.

"It has air-conditioning."

"It's too cold in the winter."

"It has heating."

Jakub edged over to Krysia. "Can't he just once say thank you?"

She smiled at her brother. "He's saying it. Look at his eyes. We'll finish soon."

"I don't understand you," he said with a shake of his

head. "You never get angry. You had to rearrange your *entire* life for him."

"He arranged his for us. Remember Sister Nathaniel? Patience is a virtue." Krysia sat next to the old man. "Every nail, screw, bit of iron—everything from your workshop is on the benches; you sort, okay? Your old tools, too. They're rusty and missing screws, but you can fix them."

Funny. Rusty and missing a screw. Like him. He couldn't suppress his laughter any longer. An explosive bray startled his guests.

"It's like your basement room but with more light," Michal chimed in.

"Tell Dziadzia what Uncle Michal found. Wait, I have a picture," Alicia said, suddenly wide awake.

She wriggled out of his lap and pulled a crushed piece of paper from under her sweater, then smoothed it. The old man looked. It was a chair. *An armchair?* There were puffy white clouds all over it.

"This is a pretty picture, Alicia. Thank you," her grandfather said.

"It's your chair, can't you tell? The broken one. It's in the garage by the TV."

It couldn't be his. But the kids were trying their best to make up for their betrayal. He forgave them. *Youngsters.* They didn't have enough years on them to understand an old man's soul.

"It's your chair, Tata. No repairs at all," Michal said.

The old man beamed at him. Every laugh, every smile became more natural. Maybe Michal *did* understand him. He had an actor's intuition.

"You have a job to do, Tata. Alicia has a dog. It will need watching when we're in school." Krysia hoped the scrap of fur she adopted from a shelter would give the old man as much pleasure as his other little dogs had. Cock-a-poos were highly intrusive in their love. Perfect.

"Let's go, family, we're wasting time," Cas announced,

getting to his feet.

The old man half stood up, then fell back. Time was money for his son the lawyer.

"I can't go. I can't fly." The darkness was returning. A prison buried in the hell of Florida.

Marcin stooped to raise the old man out of his chair. "I'm driving. I have to pick up some Seminole chickee miniatures."

Chicks? Why? Hens? Girls?

Marcin looked at the old man's puzzlement. "Little Seminole houses. Ideas for my furniture."

Seminole houses? His mind would be hopping with these kids around.

Sister Anna walked through the open door. "Don't you people ever sleep?"

"We're outta here." The old man congratulated himself. That's what young people said nowadays.

"Sign on the dotted line so we can get on the road." Cas stood before him holding a pen.

The old man read it quickly, then signed. He could say he didn't remember signing. Touched in the head was easy to play. *As long as my Krysia owns the house, I'm safe.*

*****

The old man looked behind him as they drove out of the parking lot. Sister Anna stood in the doorway, her arms hidden under the bib of her habit. He waved. She wasn't that bad, that Sister Anna. He settled his head against the headrest; Alicia's head was in his lap. She raised it and pushed another picture into his hands before falling asleep again: an entire meadow of zinnias.

Who knew? Maybe when he got old he would come back. It wasn't a bad place. Nice flowers.

About the Author

Christine Kulikowski has worked as a lab technician, actress, animal breeding and biology researcher and college instructor, grant and science writer, English literature and writing college adjunct, newspaper reporter and editor, and author of fiction. Chris' recreation has included hiking, climbing volcanoes, community theatre, dog rescue, political activism and traveling. She owns one husband, two overachieving children, two odd dogs and a cat who adopted the family last year.

How Will Santa Find Me?

Daria Ludas

The black Lexus pulled into the two-car garage. Jim Byrnes stepped out, slammed the door and unloaded the boxes from the trunk. "Three boxes and twelve long years," he said, staring into the empty trunk. He closed the trunk, dropped the boxes into a corner, and walked into the house.

He hung his keys on the key rack in the kitchen and looked at the clock. "Eleven a.m. on Friday the thirteenth. This day couldn't get any worse." He walked into the family room, looked at the granite bar and shook his head.

"Naw ... too early." He turned away, removed his tie and flung it over the leather recliner. He unbuttoned the top button of his white shirt and faced the bar again. "Ah, what the hell. Why not? Its five o'clock somewhere."

He walked over to the bar and poured a shot of Irish whiskey. He straddled a bar stool, threw back the shot and shook his head. He gazed around the room. "Well, all of this will have to go." He gazed around the room. "How am I going to tell Carolyn and Colleen we have to move?"

His cell phone vibrated to inform him of an incoming text. He removed it from his shirt pocket and stared. Carolyn. *How is your day going, Hon?*

Dandy. Just Dandy, he typed.

Are you okay? Carolyn texted back. *Having a bad day? Don't worry. It's Friday. The weekend is here! Family time. See you later. Love you.*

Love you too, Jim texted.

He placed his phone on the bar. How could he tell her he lost his job and they could no longer live the life style they had become accustomed to? He walked around the house, paused in the formal dining room, and looked up at the tray ceiling with the crystal chandelier glistening in the sunlight. He touched one of the dangling crystals. "Royal Street," he murmured. He remembered buying the antique chandelier on their anniversary trip to New Orleans.

The house had been under construction, and while browsing the antique shops they'd found the perfect fixture. *This one.* The one which hung in a French castle many years ago was theirs. The antique shop had wrapped and shipped it to their townhome with great care. The glistening crystals brought a tear to Jim's eyes. He blinked, brushed his tears away.

"I'm the man of this household, and I have to be strong when they come home," he announced to the beautiful glass tears.

He rushed up to the master suite, showered, changed clothes, and went downstairs to brew a pot of coffee. He noticed the clock. Three o'clock. They would be home soon.

He was sitting at the kitchen table sipping his coffee when he heard the garage door open. He opened the kitchen door to greet them.

"Daddy!" Four-year-old Colleen greeted him.

He lifted her up, and kissed her. "Hi, Pumpkin."

Carolyn Byrnes followed her daughter. "Hi," she

whispered kissing her husband's cheek. "Why are you home so early?"

Jim put Colleen down. "Do you want to watch your favorite show? Daddy will fix you a snack."

"Okay!"

Colleen ran into the family room and sat on the sectional sofa. Jim put the television on for her and set it to her favorite kiddie station. He returned to the kitchen and Carolyn's glare. He sliced an apple, poured a small glass of milk placed it on a tray and brought it to his daughter.

"Thank you, Daddy."

"You're welcome, honey."

He walked back to the kitchen and faced Carolyn. "We need to talk." He poured Carolyn a cup of coffee, and joined her at the table. He took her hand. "Babe, I'm sorry to tell you this, but I lost my job today."

"What? What happened?" Carolyn trembled.

"As you know, the company has been having financial trouble the last three quarters. Our earnings are way down. The owners are forced to downsize and five executives were let go today. I happen to be one of them."

Carolyn began to cry. "How awful for you. You have worked so hard for this position, and now..." She clutched his hand. "All the hours you devoted to that place. The weekends you gave up, to get ahead just to have it all taken away."

Jim patted her hand. "I'll get another job someplace. They're giving me one year severance pay. They'll continue to deposit it into our account. That's the only good news. The worst news is..."

"I know," she said, blinking away more tears.

He walked around the table to hug her. "We'll probably have to sell this." He kissed her forehead. "This was our dream house, I know. But I've been thinking..."

She grabbed a napkin and wiped her tears. "Thinking? When did you have time to think?"

He sat down. "I've been thinking since nine-thirty this morning." He sipped more coffee. "I realized we would have to downsize but that doesn't mean we can't have our dream house."

"How do you figure that, Jim?"

He dashed to the garage and brought in his briefcase. He placed a notepad and pen on the table. "I'll show you." He poured them more coffee, sat down, wrote numeric figures on the pad, and passed it to Carolyn.

She sipped her coffee and studied his notes. "So you think this is what our house would sell for?"

"Yes. The middle figure is what our current equity would be, and we could buy a smaller house for cash and have at least fifty left over to make improvements. What do you think?"

"It seems all speculative to me, Jim. I mean, it looks great on paper, but what if we don't get our price? What if we can't find something decent for less money? There are a lot of variables in this."

"I know that. That's why we need to do this now, while I'm still getting paid. They gave me a check today for my remaining vacation, personal and sick time that can be used for a down payment on another house."

"I don't think we'll find anything in Princeton for what we can afford."

"Living in Princeton has been great, but there are lovely areas in the Princeton area that we can be just as happy in." He clutched her hand. "The town we live in isn't important. What's important is that we are together. Unless—you don't want to be with me anymore. Is that it Carolyn? Do you feel like your husband is a loser now he lost his high paying job?"

"No! How *dare* you think that? I'm highly insulted that a thought like that would even enter your mind. I love you. I love our family."

Jim wiped a tear from his eye and hugged his wife. "I'm sorry. I felt demoralized today. I love you and Colleen and want the best for you two."

"Let's go talk to Colleen," Carolyn said softly, extending her hand to take his.

They carried their coffee mugs and a platter of cookies to the family room and sat on the leather sectional on each side of Colleen.

"What are you watching?" Jim asked his daughter.

"My favorite show, Daddy."

Carolyn placed a few cookies on a plate and served it to Colleen. "We want to talk to you about something."

Colleen accepted the cookies. "Thanks, Mommy..."

Jim put his arm on his daughter's shoulder. "Honey, Mommy and I have something to tell you."

Colleen chomped on her cookie. "What?"

"Daddy lost his job today and we have to move from this house."

"Why?" Colleen asked.

"Since Daddy isn't going to work for a while, we won't have enough money to stay here, so we have to sell it and buy a new one."

Colleen crossed her arms across her chest. "No, no, no. I am not moving to another house."

Jim and Colleen stared at their daughter, then glanced at each other. "Now Colleen, we have to do this." Carolyn stroked her daughter's blonde curls. "We can't stay here. We will find a house just as nice as this."

"But Christmas is coming soon. How will Santa find me?"

"We have a long time till Christmas comes," Jim assured his daughter.

"Oh no. Christmas is coming. The TV says so."

"Christmas is over three months away. We will be in a new house by then. Santa will know exactly where to find you."

Colleen scooted off the sectional and into the foyer. Carolyn and Jim ran after her. "Where are you going?" Carolyn asked,

Colleen stopped at the front door. "This is how Santa knows where I live." She pointed to the red lacquered front doors.

Jim smiled and knelt beside his daughter. "Tell you what. We will find a house that has a red front door. Than Santa will be sure to find you."

Carolyn joined her husband and daughter. "Yes, honey, Daddy and I will make sure Santa finds our new house."

"Will it have two red doors, Mommy?"

Carolyn and Jim glanced at each other. "Our new house will have a red door, Honey. Daddy promises." Jim kissed the top of his daughter's head. "Daddy promises you that."

The next morning Jim woke early, searched his computer and started making breakfast for his family. Collen ran to the kitchen. "What are you cooking, Daddy?"

Jim lifted his daughter into his arms. She smelled like baby shampoo and sleep. "Good morning. Are you ready to eat bacon, eggs and toast?"

"Yeah."

"Okay." He put her back on her little feet. "Go wake up Mommy, tell her breakfast is ready."

A few minutes later Colleen and Carolyn entered the kitchen holding hands. "Good morning." Carolyn greeted her husband with a kiss.

The family sat at the kitchen island eating their breakfast. "We are going for a ride today."

"Where Daddy, where?"

"It's a surprise," Jim said.

"When are we going?" Carolyn asked.

"As soon as we finish eating."

Half an hour later, the family pulled into a parking lot. "Look! Two red doors!" Colleen squealed from the back.

Jim turned off the ignition and turned to Colleen and Carolyn. "This is Red Door Realty. We have an appointment with a nice lady named Linda to sell our house and buy a new one."

Carolyn shot him a look. "I'm surprised you did this behind my back. I thought we made major decisions together."

Jim unhooked his seatbelt and turned to his wife. "I thought we talked this over yesterday and agreed we would have to sell the house."

"Well, yes, but you went ahead and made an appointment without telling me."

"I know, Carolyn. I searched online this morning for area realtors and when I saw the name Red Door Realty and Colleen's reaction to moving I thought I would surprise you both."

Carolyn turned to face her daughter and then her husband. "Maybe you were thinking of us, but I *don't* like surprises. You know that. Look, I'm not even dressed up. I'm in jeans and sneakers."

"It's fine. I'm in jeans, too. Let's go in."

They unhooked Colleen from her car seat and walked through the red doors. "May I help you?" the young man at the desk asked.

"Yes. We have an appointment to see Linda," Jim said.

The young man picked up the phone and paged Linda to the front desk.

A tall brunette woman wearing a navy pant suit approached them. "Hi. I'm Linda Paterson." She extended her hand and one by one, Jim, Carolyn and Colleen accepted. "Come to my office," she said with a wave of her hand.

They walked into her office, and Linda closed the red door behind them. "Please have a seat and tell me what you're looking to do."

Carolyn held Colleen on her lap and let Jim do the talking

"I just lost my job and we need to downsize. We're

hoping to get enough equity from our current home to buy something else for cash."

Colleen crossed her arms over her chest and shook her head. "I don't want to leave my house."

Linda looked at Jim and Carolyn. "Why not?"

"Christmas is coming and Santa won't know where I live."

Linda walked over to her file cabinet and pulled something out of the drawer. "Do you like to color, Colleen?"

"Yes!"

"Come here." Linda placed a Christmas coloring book and a box of crayons on the small round table in front of the loveseat. Colleen jumped off her mother's lap and ran to Linda.

"Let's find Santa in here." She turned a few pages. "Here he is. Would you color this for me, please, while I talk to Mommy and Daddy?"

Colleen grinned, selected a red crayon and started coloring Santa. Linda returned to Jim and Carolyn. "When can I come to look at your house?"

Jim and Carolyn looked at each other. "The sooner the better," Jim said.

Linda checked her watch. "How about six this evening?"

Jim and Carolyn nodded in agreement. They scooped up Colleen, who clutched the Christmas coloring book. "Take it with you and finish the Santa picture. You can give it to me tonight."

****

Promptly at six o'clock the front door bell chimed. Colleen ran to the door with the Santa picture she had finished coloring. Carolyn followed her and opened the door.

"Hi, Linda. Welcome to our home."

Linda handed Carolyn a cheesecake. "For you."

She handed Colleen a cellophane bag of oatmeal raisin cookies. "And these are for you."

"Thank you." Colleen handed Linda the Santa picture.

"Where do you want to start?" Carolyn asked.

"The foyer is good. Show me around."

"Look at the red doors." Colleen said. "That's how Santa knows where I live."

Carolyn took Colleen's hand. "Come on, let's show Linda the rest of the house."

"Where is Jim?"

"He's straightening up some things in the shed. We'll meet him in the yard."

As Carolyn guided them from room to room, the memories engulfed her. She had to fight back tears when they got to Colleen's room. How many hours she and Jim had spent picking colors and the perfect Winnie the Pooh graphics. They'd laid on the floor looking at the starlit ceiling the evening they finished it, Jim's head on her lap, discussing all the plans they had for their new daughter... They'd agreed this was their perfect home.

Linda touched her arm and smiled. "You'll make wonderful new memories in your new home, I know you will."

Together the small entourage toured the rest of the home and then the grounds, a narrative that included observations from Colleen.

"I guess it's okay if we have to move, but we really need to be sure Santa can find us," she told Linda with a very solemn face.

"We'll make sure of that, I promise," Linda replied just as solemnly.

****

Three weeks later Linda brought them a full price

offer which they accepted. "A new listing came in yesterday for a spacious split level within your price point. Would you be interested—"

Jim interrupted. "Can we see it now?"

"Now?" Linda asked.

Carolyn nodded. "Yes. Now that we have an offer on the table, we'll need to find something fast."

"Let me see what I can do." Linda pulled out her cell phone, made a call, and turned to Jim and Carolyn. "How about in an hour? The owner needs to straighten up the dinner dishes, round up the kids and head for the mall."

"An hour is great," Jim said.

Linda picked up her phone and confirmed the appointment.

"Colleen," Carolyn called. "We're going with Linda to see a house, let's get ready to go."

Colleen ran to Linda. "Does the house have a red door like our house and yours?"

Linda grinned. "I won't know until we go see it." She looked at Jim and Carolyn and shook her head.

"Come on, let's wash your hands and face and get ready." Carolyn said

An hour later Linda was turning the combination lock to the correct numbers. The silver key fell down, Linda unlocked the door and invited the family in.

"Why isn't the door red, Daddy?"

Jim bent down to his daughter. "Honey, not every door is red. You see other doors in our neighborhood that aren't red. But Daddy will paint this one so Santa will know where you live."

Jim held Colleen's hand as they toured the home. "These rooms are spacious."

"Follow me," Linda led the family to the basement. "This is a room just for Colleen."

The basement had been converted into a toy/playroom. Colleen ran to the play kitchen and started placing miniature pots and pans on the toy stove.

Carolyn ran to her. "Colleen, those aren't your toys, honey. You can't play with them."

"I play with this at my school." She looked up at Linda. "Santa is bringing me a kitchen for Christmas."

"I am sure he will." Linda said. "So what do you think?"

Jim winked at Linda. "Can we have a private moment?"

"Sure. Take your time. Go look around again. I'll stay down here with Colleen."

Fifteen minutes later Jim and Carolyn appeared. "We would like to make a full price offer. We can do cash with the price difference," Jim said. "Do you have papers with you?"

"I do. I'll have to get them from my car. Be right back."

The last Monday in November, just after Thanksgiving, Jim and Carolyn closed on both homes.

They drove to their new address where they were greeted by Linda.

"Look. The door is red! The door is red!" Colleen squealed.

They left the car and walked to the front door. Above the lacquer-painted front door hung a brass plate sign that read *Byrne Family*.

Jim lifted his daughter. "See, Colleen? I think Santa can find you now."

The family entered and invited Linda in. Colleen made a beeline to the play area in the basement, and screamed. "Mommy, Daddy hurry up! Come here!"

Jim, Carolyn and Linda ran to the basement. A brand new play kitchen and mini equipment was stationed in the same area the previous owner had, wrapped in a giant red bow with Colleen's name attached.

"Santa was here already and left this for me.' Colleen beamed.

The doorbell rang. "Must be the movers," Carolyn called over her shoulders as she ran up the steps.

Jim gazed at Linda. "Looks like you have been a mighty busy lady."

"Yes. Usually this is a slow time of year, but our office has been very busy. Seems everyone wants to get into their new homes before Christmas."

"I just want to thank you. Not only for finding us the perfect home, but for the beautiful professional looking door, door plate, and the toy kitchen."

Linda shook her head and laughed. "It was my pleasure to find your family this home. But the rest must have been Santa. I don't do doors or kitchens."

About the Author

Daria Ludas resides in New Jersey with her husband of forever. Retired from many years as an elementary school teacher, she stays busy. She's a member of Sisters-in-Crime and Liberty States Fiction Writers and her short stories have been published in several crime fiction anthologies. Her first novel, MERCIFUL BLESSINGS, co-authored with N. L. Quatrano, will be released under the pen name Lynn Kathleen in late 2015.

Not a Creature Stirred

Carol MacAllister

My friend Kathy announced, "It's your turn this year," and left the room for a moment. A spry bounce livened her walk as she returned.

She and husband Tom were sharing an empty-nester Christmas Eve with my husband and me. We picked at sweets and sipped our drinks while reminiscing past times, reviewed what we'd mailed to the kids and grandkids for gifts and when we'd visit with them next.

Empty-nesting on special times like Christmas can be especially tough on the psyche if you let it. As Kathy headed toward me, I wondered what she carried in her hands. A large picture book? How did the book tie in with her earlier pronouncement? She placed it on my lap and grinned.

"We might as well do it. Can't break the chain."

"Kath – what are you talking about?" My curiosity was piqued. "Hmm." I looked at the book's cover. *The Night Before Christmas*. It did seem fitting.

She glanced at me and then over at my husband nestled in the comfortable wing back. With a questioning expression, she asked, "Who wants to read it?"

My husband pulled back.

"I'll do it." I was always up for a little merriment.

"Great!"

My three listeners settled back as I read Moore's beautifully illustrated poem. Of course, I spoke with dramatic flair and showed each illustration. As I finished the last line, "And to all a good night," she handed me a pen.

"What's this for," I asked.

She turned to the very last page. A list of signatures lined it. Following each was a date.

"The readers," she said then pointed to the first name and date written nearly twenty-five years before. She read it aloud and scanned down the list, stopping on occasion to recall the reader, give a short remark about that particular night, laughed at the kids' signatures when they were younger and gave a sigh recalling readers who'd passed on.

I readily took up the pen and signed and dated the page. I was now a permanent part of a Christmas Eve celebration tradition.

About three years passed. Again the four of us spent an empty-nester Christmas Eve together. I looked forward to Kathy's traditional presentation.

"Now, let's see." She glanced at my husband then doubled-checked the book's last page. She handed it to him. "Your turn."

He accepted the book with obvious hesitation. "Okay."

His reading, though a bit choppy, was enjoyed. He delighted in signing and dating the page. I have to admit I, too, enjoyed peeking at my past signature and for a moment relived the fun of my special presentation.

As time does, it brought changes. We retired and moved. No longer tied to stateside, our first Christmas away was worse than being an empty-nester. No family or friends to share in the holidays. But two years later when my son's second family presented us with a new grandchild, we hopped on a flight to the States eager to share in our new grandson's Christmas.

And what did I bring along as a gift? A lovely illustrated copy of *The Night Before Christmas*. Easy to pack and time-tested.

That Christmas Eve, I presented the book. I explained the beginning of a new tradition for the family. "Grandpa and I will read the poem to you this year."

The three mature grandchildren who'd returned home for the night liked the idea. We all sat around the dining room table. This time "Grandma and Grandpa" took turns reading the poem to everyone, with lots of flair to everyone's delight. Eyes and ears fixated – not a creature stirred – not even a mouse!

When we got to the last line, everyone spoke the words together: "Merry Christmas to all, and to all a good night." The baby clapped his hands. Even at eighteen months, he sat quietly and attentive, maybe sensing the feel of family.

Of course after the older grandkids noted that we signed and dated the last page, they vied for reading positions for the upcoming years. The oldest, a college junior, petitioned for the next reading, stating she might not be around to read it after next year. The other two agreed and then assigned themselves future time slots.

Right now, the book is tucked away for the next presentation. Hopefully, like Kathy's book, our new family tradition will continue through many upcoming holidays. The next arriving generation, and perhaps even a third, will enjoy listening to the timeless poem. They'll get a kick out of seeing their signatures and those of others from the past. As individual thoughts touch back to particular nights, readers' voices will speak in memories.

As each holiday comes along, all will celebrate the occasion. And if each listens carefully, they'll hear the full chorus of readers' whispers. Voices mixed in the traditional refrain wishing everyone a Merry Christmas.

About the Author

Carol MacAllister's short stories are published in multiple genre and poetry anthologies. THE BLACK-MOOR TALES ebook is a well-reviewed collection of her work. She holds an MFA in Creative Writing, has won numerous competitions and awards, and has completed her third novel, a YA historical coming of age romance, working title Evening Star. Her novel, THE MAYAN CALENDAR REVEAL eBook was released on December 21, 2012-a significant date to be sure. Thank you to Nancy Quatrano for another entertaining publication.

A Day's Tale

Richard Masterson

The temperature on that cold Christmas Eve in 1941 dropped to a little past minus ten degrees, and the wind didn't help. The snow hung in the air like a fine mist; not only could you smell it but you could taste it.

Peddling along the lake road with the rhythmic squeaks and rattles of the old bike, Jim looked up at the heavy white clouds and thought, *maybe we'll have snow*. His thoughts drifted back to what his brother said before getting on the bus to Fort Dix.

"Keep the chain well oiled, Jim, and you might get another year out of this bike. I'll be back when the war's over and maybe we'll build you a new one."

Back when the war's over, Jim thought. He didn't know too much about wars. But what he did know was that this Christmas he would be away from home, staying with his old Aunt Hattie in Lakewood, New Jersey.

Jim's mother, a widow, had landed a job with Ford Motors, now a defense plant in Mahwah. With his brother in the Army, Jim was all alone. And at fourteen, his mother wanted him to stay with his aunt on a farm that had gone broke during the Great Depression. Those plans all came about after December 7th, when a place he never heard of was bombed by the Japanese.

Aunt Hattie lived off of the Government. She received a monthly welfare check, plus a ration book for groceries, forcing her to count every penny. So there would be no Christmas tree or decorations, which meant no presents *under* the tree.

But Jim knew of his aunt's situation from stories his mother told him. He would have to adjust to his new life style, as sad as it would be. There were no other kids around his age that he could play with, only the animals on the farm; a dozen chickens that scratched around the property.

****

On the morning of Christmas Eve, Aunt Hattie called Jim into the kitchen. She reached up and took down a teapot from the pantry.

"Jimmy, I need you to go to the store in town. I need a few things... you remember how to get there, don't ya?"

"Yes," he said, "I just follow the lake road right into Main Street...and then turn on Second Ave."

"Very good, you do remember! Please don't lose it, this is all we have till the first of the month."

She opened the closet and took out a woolen scarf. "Here! Wrap this around your neck and keep your Mackinaw buttoned...ooh, and yes, here's the shopping list, put it with the ration book in your top shirt pocket and make sure it's buttoned. The man will ask you for the ration book before you give him the money, make sure he gives it back to you, you understand?"

Jim nodded.

"When you're done, come right home. No dallying, there's snow in the air.

Jim checked the chain and tires on the bike. Going

down the driveway, he waved to his aunt.

"Make sure you count the change," she hollered back from the front porch.

Even with the scarf wrapped around him, the cold air cut into his face; his nose felt numb. The shortest way to town would be to cut through the abandoned cranberry bogs.

The cranberry farmers went broke after the bank foreclosed on them along with the shacks that the workers lived in alongside of the wagon road. The bogs were located in the swampy lowlands of the pine forest that cut a half mile off the trip. Bucking the cold wind with his head bowed, he continued on until he came to the rutted wagon road and then made the turn.

Halfway through the bogs, he heard the cry of what sounded like an animal. He stopped and listened. Again he heard it. Sounded like dog. Jim whistled.

"Where are ya, boy?" he hollered. No response. He whistled again.

A loud bark came from the frozen culvert that ran through the bog for drainage. He laid his bike down, looked down into the ditch and saw a big black Labrador tangled in the briars, struggling to free himself. In the dog's struggle the briars cut deep into his legs.

Jim slid down the icy bank and approached the dog. The briars were tightly wrapped around the dog's legs and the struggling to get out made the situation worse.

"Okay, boy, take it easy now," Jim said. "Let me help ya."

The more the big dog struggled to free himself, the tighter the briars became. Jim remembered what his brother told him about injured animals.

"Be careful Jim, they become frightened, and will bite you for self-protection. They could not only give you a serious bite, but they could be rabid."

Jim reached out to the dog and stroked his head.

"Good boy, good boy, everything will be all right, good boy."

He took out his pocket knife and with great care, cut the briars around the dog's leg. Then, gently, he helped the dog to his feet and onto the roadside. The dog began to shiver with the blood seeping out of the cuts on his legs.

Jim petted the big dog. "You'll be okay, boy. Where's your collar?" *With no collar, he's got to be a stray.*

He had no time for the injured dog now, but he knew, in time, the dog's wounds would heal. Right now he had to get to the store. He got back on his bike and started for town again. Halfway up the road, he turned around and gave the dog a last look, only to find the poor creature limping after him at a half trot.

Ah, the poor thing. I hope he gets tired and stops to rest. Maybe by picking up speed I can lose him. No, that's not right. He might hurt himself trying to keep up. I just can't think about it now. Maybe on the way back, I'll check to see if he's still there.

Over the stone bridge and on to Main Street, Jim rode another block and made a left onto Second Street. He parked his bike under the green awning that read, "The Great Atlantic and Pacific Tea Company," and walked toward the store.

He spotted something out of the corner of his eye. The battered black dog came limping over and lay down under the awning. He began licking his wounds. Jim walked back and took out his bandana and wiped the blood from the dog's leg, then put it back in his pocket. With a soft whimper, the dog reached over and licked Jim's hand.

"Just lie here," Jim said, "I'll be right out." He entered the store, letting the screen door slam behind him, welcoming the warmth of the store and the aroma of fresh ground coffee.

He had only put a few items in the basket when the

barking started. The sound came from outside the store. *Oh, no....*

The barking grew louder, alerting the tall clerk, who walked over to the front window and looked outside. He turned to the people in the store. "Does anyone here own a big black dog?" he hollered in annoyance.

Jim kept his head down, ignoring the clerk, afraid someone might have seen him with the dog. Sure enough–

"I think the dog belongs to that kid over there," the bald headed man with the glasses and the pointed nose said, nodding toward Jim. "I saw the dog follow him in on his bike."

The barking grew louder with a fierce tone.

The clerk walked over to Jim and stared down at him. "Is that your dog out there kid?" he bellowed.

Jim looked over the partition and saw a large crowd had gathered outside, forming a circle around the dog.

"Not really," Jim replied. He became scared and decided to leave the store and abandon the groceries *and* the dog. Maybe he could come back later and the dog would be gone.

He left the basket and headed for the screen door. Looking out, he saw the large crowd had increased around the dog that was now barking louder with a menacing snapping growl that kept the crowd at bay.

Jim quickly walked toward his bike and gave the dog one last look of denial. Then he stopped when he noticed the dog was standing over what looked like a piece of crumpled paper. He took a closer look.

Lordy, it was a twenty-dollar bill! Jim pulled out his bandanna, stuck his hand into his pocket and came up empty. *Oh my God, that's Aunt's money. It must have dropped out when I pulled out my bandanna earlier.*

Jim walked through the crowd, knelt down and picked up the twenty-dollar bill and put it in his pocket. Wrapping his arms around the dog's head and stroking it, Jim pulled the dog close.

"Good boy, good dog," he said, as he stroked him again and again.

The dog limped back and laid down under the awning. Jim walked back into the store. When the screen door slammed, he heard someone in the dwindling crowd say, "Must be an early Christmas present."

As Jim carefully counted his change and tucked the precious coupon book into his top pocket and buttoned it, he smiled. *Christmas, eh? A great name for a great dog.*

About the Author

Richard is a retired Newark, NJ, police sergeant who enjoys writing his memories in the form of powerful short stories. He's currently working on a mystery short story for the East Coast Mystery collection. We are delighted that he's chosen to share this holiday memory with SNOWBIRD readers. He can be emailed at rmasterson34@comcast.net.

A Very Blessed Christmas

Jack Owen

Bobby McCain's finger traced deep down the Christmas term exam results list, posted on the cork bulletin board in the main entrance to school, before he found his own name.

"I think you've broken a record *bbb-Bobby*," Nicholas Pond's familiar falsetto voice piped up behind him, accompanied by a chorus of snickering classmates. "You're bottom of the class, again. What is that? Six times now? Are you trying for the *Guinness Book of Records*?

The snickers welled into a wall of laughter as Bobby pushed his way through to escape the humiliation. His mind ran through a series of snappy responses but, unless he sang it, his tongue-tied stutter would merely increase his anguish.

"Got you on the run again, eh?" boomed Jerry Stenopolis, his desk mate, when he ducked into the sanctuary of the library. There, quiet reigned under the rule of Miss Thorneapple's hissed shushing to any who dared break the command of the large sign above her desk: SI-LENCE.

"Sssshhhhhhh!"

"Old cow," Jerry mouthed behind the cover of an atlas which concealed a copy of the girlie magazine *Playmate*. Though of similar age to Bobby within a few weeks, the rotund chunky boy already sported a five o'clock shadow, hairy arms, chest and an endowment which was the envy of the locker room.

"I wouldn't mind so much if I could just fire back at him," Bobby squeaked in a sing-song pre-adolescent voice. Jerry, bulky enough to thump anyone who teased his swarthy appearance, smiled good naturedly, joining in the instant shushing sounds issuing from Miss Thornapple's direction.

Bobby smiled back. He focused on the marked pages of the hymnal, memorizing marked passages where the choir would accompany the soloist.

Sung, of course, by the teacher's pet, top of the class and prize-winning soprano, Nicholas. It was a role which could have gone to Bobby. But he could neither introduce nor laud dignitaries and the choirmaster before the big Christmas concert final with his stuttering.

Bobby's perfect pitch was discovered, buried in the ranks of children assembled in the school's auditorium prior to classes starting, by the patrolling music master monitoring for mischief makers.

Mr. Jewell's ears actually twitched when he heard the dulcet tones of Bobby's crystal clear voice above the mumbled jumble of the massed bodies reciting words by rote.

He was crushed when he singled the boy out after assembly, to get his name.

"Bb-bb-b Bobby Cccc-cc-Cain, sssir."

"Goodness, you stutter, boy?"

Bobby glanced around at the vacant assembly hall and, using the sing-song voice he only employed at home or with close friends, nodded agreement.

"Mum says it's nerves. Dad says it's stupid and I

should go to a school for the Deaf and the Daft. I don't know why, but I can sing fine," he gushed in one breath.

"That's unfortunate. But you have a splendid voice, and I can use you in the choir. We go on trips, to other schools to perform. To churches, even Canterbury Cathedral, once, y'know," Jewell coaxed.

Bobby's eyes lit up. He had never been outside the town limits or left the confines of the Sussex seaside resort of Eastbourne. His dad sometimes took him to the pub to sing "Danny Boy", which caused some grown men to weep in their beer. Bobby pocketed a few pennies and Dad downed an extra pint, or three.

Bobby's addition to the choir as alternate soloist to Nicholas, the fair-haired diva who primped and pouted until he got his way, was a mixed blessing for both Mister Jewell and Bobby.

As Christmas term reached its conclusion the animus between the formerly ignored bottom of the class boy reached a peak when Bobby was assigned a stand-in role to offset any ailment "Star" Nicholas might suffer. Consequently both boys spent additional hours in each other's' company receiving personal coaching from the choirmaster. Nicholas resented sharing his role and Bobby, who seldom received any attention other than ridicule, responded to the tutoring and praise to the point that use of his sing-song responses diminished in Mister Jewell's presence.

It was a contrast to class work. Bobby was never called upon by teachers to supply answers to questions, following their first encounter. The disruption to discipline, when classmates dissolved into paroxysms of laughter while the tongue-tied boy struggled to respond, occupied too much time and effort to risk it again.

Three days before school ended for the holidays, and after prizes and awards were distributed to academic and sporting achievers, the school body, parents, local dignitaries and the press assembled at St. Andrews

Church for the final service of the school year.

Everything went swimmingly from the rousing choruses of "Onward Christian Soldiers" to "For Those in Peril on the Sea" to the schoolboy version of "While Shepherds Washed Their Socks By Night", until the grand finale boys' choir soprano solo, "Bless This House."

The Reverend Francis Boyce introduced choirmaster Jewell who, in turn offered his thanks to the choir and coaxed the angelic fair-haired, rosy-cheeked soloist Nicholas Pond to stand before the altar. Without benefit of microphone every syllable of the boy's introduction to the popular interdenominational hymn, rang clear throughout the massive arched church reaching every corner of the congregation.

An opening musical chord broke the hushed silence as organist Miss Priscilla Wentworth's skinny legs manipulated the organ pedals and her bony fingers pressed yellowed ivory-faced keys.

Bless this house O Lord we pray

To the discerning ear there was a slight quaver to the last note. Choirboys flinched and those who could, raised one eyebrow.

Make it safe by night and Daaay

Bless these walls so FIRM and stOUut

Nicholas's voice cracked. For a moment the stunned congregation could not believe what it heard. The anticipated pristine crystal clear sound was shattered by a fog-horn blast from hell.

Mister Jewel's face turned ashen.

Pupils, busy whispering in the pews under cover of the physical assault of the pipe organ's output and swelling chorus of the choir, hesitated. They paused, like rabbits caught in an open field under the eagle glare of a predatory bird when Nicholas's piercing tone brayed like a billy goat in pain.

While the pipe organist played on unaware, the voice-box of Nicholas Cain ranged far and wide from somewhere below his kneecaps to his crown of perfectly coiffed hair. The halo began to shake as blood drained from his face..

A nervous giggle from the plump wife of the mayor in the front pew was echoed by a gangly red-haired girl in baggy gymslip uniform a few rows behind. And her friend, and her friend's friend until a ripple of giggles ran from row to row where they washed up against the stained glass window-studded walls of the church before bouncing back. Even the thunderous sound of the heavy bass organ pipes could not conceal the laughter as Nicholas's breaking adolescent voice debuted before an audience of hundreds.

Moments before the entire sacred service dissolved into complete bedlam, a piercing soprano note, sufficient to shatter the fine crystal goblet of wine on the altar, cut through the hubbub.

"Keeping want and troubles out"

A new voice, with finely enunciated words pierced the raucous audience like a laser beam, penetrated brains and struck a chord in the hardest of hearts.

In that moment Bobby McCain experienced the thrill of stilling a mass audience for the first time in his life. His choirmaster became a believer in prayer. And, into the stunned silence, before Bobby launched the next verse, his desk mate broke wind in a laudatory loud and noxious way – emptying a circle of seats ten feet in all directions – while the media had a field day.

By the time Bobby got home that night, the fair-haired Nicholas was relegated to distant memory, while recordings of the singing stutterer went viral, worldwide. For Bobby and his family, it was the most blessed Christmas at the McCain house, ever.

About the Author

Englishman Jack Owen reported news for local, regional and national publications on both sides of the Atlantic, before becoming a short-story writer and book author. Enquiring minds can Google, Amazon.com and FaceBook his career, blogs, media exposure and current capers and, on a good day, have a chinwag.

Daddy for the Long Haul

Nancy Quatrano

"Mommy," I asked for the sixth time in five minutes, "is Daddy going to be home for Christmas?"

She wiped her hands on her faded bib apron and swiped away toast crumbs from the enameled table in our kitchen. Then she looked at me and gave me a tired smile.

"He called last night and said that if he could get through Buffalo before the snowstorm hit, he'd be here. He wants to, Lynne, but I don't know. Maybe we need to pray it doesn't snow."

I hung my five-year old head and thought about that. I liked snow. I often sat curled in the window seat in my room, watching the snow turn the willow branches into glittering fairy sticks. No snow for Christmas? Maybe that would be okay. If Daddy wouldn't be home, Christmas wouldn't be the same.

Mom tapped me on the shoulder. "Why don't you go up to your playroom for a little while? Don't worry, it will all be all right."

I dragged my feet up the two flights of stairs to the

playroom in the attic where my rocking horse waited beside Eddie's playpen. My little brother wasn't old enough to let loose so he stayed in the playpen. I got to watch him while I rode.

I threw my red felt cowgirl hat to the floor and climbed into the wooden saddle. That black and white horse always knew how I felt and gently rocked me back and forth until I felt better. Sometimes, when I was in my red hat and cowgirl skirt though, he threw me off and made me laugh. He was my best friend. Except for Daddy.

"Trigger, we need to make sure it doesn't snow too much for Daddy to come home, okay?" I whispered in his wooden ear.

My horse rocked and rocked as I talked to him, until my mother appeared in the doorway with my brother in her arms. He grinned when he saw me and reached out his chubby little arms. I was in charge of Eddie until Mom got dinner finished. I knew the drill.

I heard the telephone ring just before Mom came and got us to come to the kitchen. "Was that Daddy?" I asked as I pulled out the chrome-legged chair and climbed up.

"No, that was your Uncle Sal. He's coming by tonight to set up your father's train set for Christmas. We might as well trim that tree while he's here, too. Your dad will tired when he finally makes it home."

I knew better than to argue, but I wanted to. Uncle Sal was doing all of Daddy's stuff. I had trouble making my food go down my throat. Something was in there.

I helped Mom clean up the kitchen while my brother played on the floor in the dining room next door. He was starting to crawl and he was practicing on the hard wood floors by hanging onto my big toy trucks and scooting along behind them as they slid along.

"Don't you break those, Ed," I yelled in my big-sister voice. He just smiled his toothless grin. I sighed. Being a big sister wasn't all that easy.

My Uncle Sal came through the back door, yelling, "Ho, ho, ho." He and Mom set up the huge sheets of plywood on the dining room table which for a few weeks, would be a winter wonderland for Daddy's trains.

Small snow-capped Christmas trees lined the tracks and trestles, and little villages sprung up on the white fluffy cloth that was supposed to be snow. Just before we were put to bed, Mom let me pull out all the people who would stand on the train station platform and walk on the snowy streets of Train Town.

"Goodnight, Uncle Sal," I said as I headed for the staircase. "The town looks really nice. Almost as nice as when Daddy does it."

He grabbed me and held me in the air over his head and shook me like a rag doll. "Who do you think taught your father to do this stuff?" Then we rubbed noses and he put me on the floor. "Your Dad will be here, Lynne. Not to worry, okay?"

I nodded. "Okay. Will you be here on Christmas, too?"

"You betcha, but not too early. Your Aunt Meg doesn't like to rush around on Christmas. We are all at church so late on Christmas Eve, we should all sleep, right?"

"I'm going to wear my red velvet dress and black shoes," I told him. "And Mom is going to curl my hair, too."

He laughed. "You'll be the prettiest of all, Baby Girl."

****

We dressed up after Christmas Eve dinner and drove to the church and Daddy still wasn't home. The snow was falling non-stop. I was sure he wouldn't make it. I asked the baby Jesus to help Daddy get home.

When we got home from the church service I ran upstairs and changed into my pink pajamas with the feet attached. Eddie was put straight to bed but I was going to wait for Daddy.

"Lynne, you get into bed, too," Mom said. "Your dad will get back here as soon as he can. I don't really think it will be tonight, though. I'm not sure if Santa could find his way in this storm."

I laughed. "Of course he can! He has Rudolph."

I fell asleep that night upstairs in the playroom with my arms wrapped around my wooden horse. I heard Mom calling me in the morning.

"Where are you, girl?" she yelled up the stairs. I scrambled to my feet and went to the narrow doorway at the top of the stairs.

"Merry Christmas, Mom," I said. "Is Eddie up yet?"

"He is. And he's not happy about waiting for you."

I ran down all of the stairs to the dining room where Train Town and the tree stood. The train was chugging around the track as puffs of smoke came out of the stack on the engine. The lights on the tree were magical and even the angel looked prettier than before.

I looked at the colorful packages beneath the tree and got on my knees. "Wow, Mom! You and Santa were busy!"

"And what about me? Did you think I'd forget?" boomed a voice from the kitchen.

"Daddy!!!!!!!!!!!!" I screamed and almost ran into him as he came in the room with his coffee. "Did you bring a new one? Did you? What color is this one?"

He laughed. "Is that the only gift you want? We should give the others away?"

I looked at the floor. "No, I'm sorry. But I just love them. When I grow up, I'm going to be a trucker, too."

He nodded, then vanished. In a minute he returned with a large red metal tractor trailer truck that I could ride and ride all year long, around and around the kitchen-dining room hallway.

Of all the gifts I ever received over the years, those metal trucks were the best.

About the Author

Published in short and full-length fiction as both Nancy Quatrano and N. L. Quatrano, this author adores mysteries with a bit of happily-ever-after thrown in. Her first full-length mystery, an RPLA Award winner, MURDER IN BLACK AND WHITE was released in August of 2015. She's an instructor, freelance writer and micro-publisher, and owner of On-Target Words, a professional writing business. She can be contacted at nancy@ontargetwords.com.

A Toy for Jess

Mark Reasoner

Bartram's Toys was the best place to find a most special Christmas present. That's what its website said and Sam Davis believed it. His parents introduced him to the store many years earlier when they lived in the old town.

Today, Sam lived another county over, but still came to Bartram's to buy presents. As an adult, he'd found great things for his child over the years, just like his father had.

And like his dad, Sam found great things for himself, too.

So when Walt Davis told him Jess's present from Grandpa and Grandma would be a gift card to the local mall this year, Sam said no.

"Not a chance, Pop," Sam told his father, "We'll go over to Bartram's. They're sure to have something special. And I promise, Dad, if we can't find anything for Jess there, you can do the gift card thing. Okay?"

Like there's any chance of that, Sam thought.

When Walt agreed, father and son made the two hour drive.

"May I help you find something?" the young clerk asked as they walked in the store.

"No, we'll just look around for now," Sam said.

The store was filled with every imaginable toy. Larger items hung from the ceiling over several rows of tall shelves packed with boxes of action figures, board games, computer games and accessories. The men moved along the aisles, looking at different things. For both of them, it was part shopping excursion and part memory lane.

"What about this, Dad?" Sam asked, holding up a radio controlled race car.

Walt shook his head smiling. "I don't think so. Jess might like it, but it's way beyond my skills. I'd never be able to help or play with it."

"Come on, Dad," Sam said, "You're not *that* old."

"But I am that bad with modern technology," Walt said. "Besides, Jess likes the old style."

The two men wandered on.

Bartram's special collection area took up space just outside the stockroom. Antique toys, collectibles and other valuables filled those shelves. Some things dated to the nineteenth century and most were from days before World War Two. The Davises slowly looked around.

Walt looked at antique cars and trucks, while Sam wandered through the space, looking over everything. Then he joined his father.

"Wow, Dad," he said. "I never knew these old things would cost so much."

"Good things are made to last," Walt said. "I remember some of these."

Sam took a very realistic looking metal fire engine from the shelf. He looked it over, noticing the price on the bottom.

"Jess would love this," he said, "It'll be a stretch, but I think we can handle it. What do you think, Dad?"

The old man looked at the toy his son was holding and froze.

"Oh my God," he said quietly. Then he turned away so his son wouldn't see his trembling lip. Tears filled Walt's eyes.

Seeing the old man's reaction, the clerk came over. "Are you all right sir? Can I help?"

"No," Walt replied, trying to compose himself. "I'll be okay."

Sam put his hand on his father's shoulder.

"What's wrong, Dad?" he asked.

"Son," Walt said, "Let's leave this to Santa. I'm pretty sure your little one will get that fire truck for Christmas."

He walked away.

"Dad, what are you talking about?" Sam asked as he followed his father out of the store.

Outside, the two men sat on a bench. Nothing was said as Walt stared down at the sidewalk. Sam looked at his father.

"Dad, what's going on?"

"I told you I remembered those toys," the old man said. "And I do, mostly because I played with some of them. That fire truck in particular."

He turned to face his son. "I still have that one. It's up in our attic. I've saved it since I was a child. It was one of my favorites."

"That's great, Dad," Sam said, "But so what?"

"I saved it to give to you," Walt said, "but I never did."

"Why not?"

"Because I was selfish. By the time you were old enough to play with it, people started talking about how valuable things like that could be, especially if they were still in their original boxes. So I held onto it, thinking I might have something, instead of giving it to you to enjoy."

"I even had this silly notion of hauling it to the Antiques Roadshow," Walt continued. "And you know, have that goofy guy in the Hawaiian shirt gush over it. Can you imagine?"

Sam laughed at the image.

"I guess I thought money was more important than memory," Walt said. "I loved that truck and I had some great times playing with it.

"But I guess things changed." The old man turned away and hung his head. "I'm sorry, son, I should have given the truck to you. Then you could have created your own memories."

"It's okay, Dad," Sam said, putting his arm around his father's shoulder.

"It will be," Walt replied, "It will be. I didn't pass that toy or the memories along to you, but I can certainly pass them down to Jess."

"Dad," Sam said, "knowing your granddaughter, she won't want to play with anything else Christmas morning."

About the Author

Mark Reasoner is a Hoosier by birth, a teacher by profession and a storyteller by nature. His writings have appeared in Folio Weekly, the DeKalb Literary Arts Journal and the Florida Times Union. He is also the author of the novel ONE LAST KICKOFF. He lives and writes in Neptune Beach, Florida.

Waiting for Jingle Bells

Drew Sappington

Santa took him a swig, sitting among the tombstones on Christmas Eve. It was the custom, after all, and people kind of expected you to take a nip or two waiting outside on a cold night. His starched-cloth face mask hung around his neck now, the wisps of cotton beard and hair sticking out at odd angles, the face gone bright orange over the years. He gulped fresh air, exhaled little clouds. His face was sweaty and freezing in the frigid air; too hot with the mask on, too cold with it off. The red stocking cap was pulled over his ears, functional tonight. The red suit was pulled over a couple of flannel shirts and a pair of dungarees, the shiny black leggings wrapped over cowboy boots with thick socks underneath. Santa kicked those boots a little, trying to get back the feeling in his toes.

Some years Santa sweltered in the heat, the raggedy wool suit itching, sweat dripping. There was a hard freeze tonight though, bad for the orange groves but good for that Christmas-feeling thanks to Yankee propaganda. If you had to have one or the other, frost was probably better than heat for Santas stuck in the church yard waiting for their cue. It was easier to layer-up than to tone down a wool suit.

A hymn came through the little church's windows, "Oh Come, Oh Come, Emanuel". So the service had started at last, but there was still plenty of time before his appearance. He stomped around the cemetery a little, beat his arms, trying to get his blood moving. He could have waited in his truck, kept the heater going, instead of out here in the cold. But what if some kids had showed up late, seen Santa kicked back with his mask off? No, he waited out of sight like all the Santas, his predecessors, had done. Putting up with the cold was just part of it, part of the rent you paid for the good stuff.

He moved among the tombstones. There was no path, but he was able to see well enough in the dark to keep off of folks' graves. At least the ones he knew about, the ones who still had stones or cast iron markers. The cast iron markers, the Maltese crosses, they belonged to the Confederate veterans. The Seminole War veterans had stones with the letters almost worn away. The really old graves were marked only with seashells, tokens of the pilgrim way. The small stones, with lambs or weeping cherubs, they were for children, babies. There were a lot of those in the old section.

He supposed you could argue that spending an evening in a cemetery was more suitable for Halloween than for Christmas. But this wasn't that kind of cemetery. He was among friends here, maybe more so than when they were above ground. This cemetery always felt like Christmas, even before the Santa gig, because it was one of the times of year he made it a point to visit Sarah. They had spent forty-seven years bickering with each other. For five years now he hadn't had anyone to set him straight. He glanced at her stone, but didn't stop, because he had been there earlier in the day putting a Christmas bouquet on top of her grave. He'd have to come back in a day or two to retrieve it, didn't look good to have dead plants all over the place.

He stamped his way back over towards the little church, hugging himself for warmth. He looked in a window, saw the familiar dark paneled wood walls with white trim, the ornate pot-bellied stove, the crude wooden benches.

There was a Christmas tree in the far corner, cedar branches creating halos around the old fashioned lights. A teenager was reading the Bible at the lectern that served as a pulpit. He couldn't make out the words that were being spoken, but he could see a couple of children dressed up as Mary and Joseph kneeling beside a doll in an orange-crate manger. So they had gotten the Holy Family to Bethlehem already, but no shepherds or angels yet. He still had a good wait. He didn't recognize the teenager or the children by the manger, which meant that they were ringers imported from a slightly bigger church in the nearest town.

"Away in a Manger" drifted out through the glass. He had a few mangers scattered around his place, except he called them feed troughs, but mostly he just chunked stuff on the ground for the livestock. "The cattle are lowing." Yeah, probably so, up among the scrub oak in the northwest corner, huddling together, trying to get the frost off their backs. He'd have to put up a barn for them one of these days.

He ducked under some branches, brushed aside the Spanish moss, as he moved towards John's grave. Gone a long time now, still probably the best friend he'd had. John would drive up on a Saturday, Sarah scowling at the dust cloud long before the old Ford could be identified, knowing who was coming, knowing where they were going.

"Mr. Potterson," John would say to the sometime Santa, "I was just a'heading into town, wondered if you needed to run in for anything."

"Why yes, Mr. Samuel," he would reply, "I believe I do need to pick up a few things, and I would appreciate a ride."

They would ride off together, buy a few supplies, visit with the boys on the bench in front of the feed store.

Then driving back, passing the Wishing Tree Bar, Mr. Samuel would always say, as though struck with a sudden thought, "Mr. P., would you be thirsty by any chance?"

"Thirsty? Well, you know, now that you mention it, I believe I am a little on the dry side."

"Do you suppose, Mr. P., they might have something in the Wishing Tree that could fix us up?"

"Well now, I wouldn't be surprised if they did. I guess we could check and see."

And the next Saturday, second verse same as the first.

The Wishing Tree was still there, and Sarah wasn't around to object, but stopping at the bar just wasn't the same any more. Santa tipped a little of his flask out onto old John's grave, wished him a Merry Christmas. Took another pull himself by way of a toast. He read John's stone again, a name and a couple of dates, the first one eighteen something or other. He'd never had any idea John was that old until he'd seen that marker.

Back to the window to check, keeping in the shadows, couldn't let himself be seen too early. "Hark The Herald Angels Sing," little girls with tinfoil wings stood behind the Holy Family now. He rubbed his cheeks, blew into his gloved hands, tried to deflect warm breath back on his face. Man, that temperature was still dropping. He pulled the cloth mask back over his face to keep the night air off for a bit. Couldn't leave it on too long, though. Wouldn't do to start sweating again. He arranged the wisps of beard, wandered off away from the window.

He could barely hear it, coming from the church. "There's a star in the sky, there's a song in the air..."

He looked up through the branches, into the still cold night. There certainly was a star in the sky, maybe a million of them, brilliant, maybe one of them the star, the star that had guided the wise men. Maybe that big one over there, in that patch of sky between the trees. "The star rains its fire while the beautiful sing..." He moved back towards the little building, peeked in the windows again. Shepherds standing behind the Family, angels behind the shepherds, the tableau moving towards completion.

It might be nice to be inside, listening to that story again. But he knew it pretty well, and that building was probably overheated, stuffy. He'd be inside soon enough, and long enough. There was a time when he had appreciated an excuse to be outside the church looking in. He and John, they were always there on work days, fixing up the roof, putting up a new outhouse, hauling off a fallen tree, while the women hoed the weeds out of the cemetery, scrubbed off the tombstones, planted a few periwinkles or marigolds around the church. Come Sunday though, the women had the building to themselves more times than not, except for Easter and Christmas.

"I do believe you have a secular sensibility, Mr. P.," John had teased him.

"Why, I believe you may have one of those yourself, Mr. S.," he had replied. Well, these days he tried to be there on Sundays. But it was nice to be out here tonight, listening to the music, watching the story, sensing it come alive again.

The wise men, bathrobes a little too long, golden pasteboard crowns sitting all angles on their heads, shifted from foot to foot in the back of the church, wise enough to wait for their proper moment. "We Three Kings..." King and God and Sacrifice.

Time to check Santa's sack. He pulled out a little cellophane bag. It had an apple, two candy canes, three pieces of hard candy and a chocolate-covered cherry.

The apple would probably be sticky by the time it got home. He was supposed to give every kid in the place a bag, the grown-ups too, if they wanted one. He put it back, pulled out a small wrapped package, shook it. It would have either a pen or a handkerchief inside. Every child would get one of these too, but there wouldn't be enough for the grown-ups.

Most of the kids were probably a bit puzzled by the little gifts these days. They got electronic gizmos and all kinds of fancy stuff, couldn't get excited about a handkerchief. But there were still some children, thin and clinging to parents with deep-lined faces, who would light up at the gifts. This was all the Christmas they were going to get. And so one Santa or another had been hanging out in the cemetery since the Santa suit was new, since the mask was jolly with ruddy cheeks, since the beard was fluffy.

"Silent Night." Almost time. He hoisted the sack on his back. He walked towards the gate, eased it open, tried to keep it from clanging when it swung shut. The congregation switched to "Jingle Bells." *Show time.*

"Ho! Ho! Ho!"

The word "miracle" gets overused around Christmas time. But this was, at least, a remarkable thing. An old man in a ragged suit and a frightening orange countenance and whiskey breath walked out of a graveyard and up the steps to the little church. And Santa Claus came in the door.

About the Author

Drew Sappington has worked as a college professor, clinical psychologist and pest control guy. He has published Hidden History of St. Augustine, one textbook, forty articles in professional psychology journals, and a few pieces in outlets that people actually read. He can be reached via email at drewsappington@msn.com.

Snowbirds in Reverse

Claire Sloan

History is only what you can remember, someone said, and my memory is as unforgiving as sliding on crushed grape skins. I refer to my snowbird Christmas in reverse.

My friend Barbara and I had long talked about going to Europe together as we had done during the summer of our freshman college year. We decided to do a bicentennial celebration of our trip, although not in the hot summer. For me, at least, Christmas would fall in a more traditional climate, no Florida Saint Nick sweating in his Santa suit, nor *ersatz* snow in St. Augustine's malls.

We arrived in Paris on a Saturday morning, exhilarated to be there, together, for the first time since college days. Our *charming boutique* hotel was on the left bank, short blocks from the Seine and The Louvre. That part of the brochure description was accurate, though "charming" would not have been my adjective of choice after the first day. We quickly discovered that the hotel's single virtue was its location.

In the prejudice of my youth, I believed that many French have a dubious trait of denying with believable sincerity what you *and they* know to be true. And if this weren't enough, they would refute the issue while treating you like an "Ugly American:" imperious, demanding, uncouth, and unappreciative. My fifty-year-old prejudice was temporarily resurrected upon arrival. If it weren't for a new friend in Provence, and Barbara's old friend, who encouraged me to recuperate at her thatched house in Normandy, our mattress experience would have spoiled the memories of Christmas in France. But, I'm getting ahead of myself.

The elevator required us to ride in shifts to our fifth floor room because two small suitcases and two thin people couldn't fit in it simultaneously. Our room was small – one had to climb over the suitcases – and the beds were narrow, almost cot sized, but sleeping arrangements seemed to be manageable. We were in Paris! In fact, everything was manageable...or so I thought.

When our tea cup sized chamber had been remodeled – perhaps fifty years ago – to include a small tub, basin, and toilet, all was carved from the already tiny room. It became necessary to suck in one's stomach in order to turn around.

The miniscule WC didn't allow the door to open inward; instead, it opened into the tiny room, clearing the side of my bed by the diameter of a guitar string. It didn't clear my legs, however, because our cot-sized beds also served as a desks, make-up tables, and chaises. Thus, I was always in the ideal spot for purple shin bruises until one of us suggested that whoever leaves the bathroom should knock twice and wait for the all clear. But who remembers to knock when leaving, not entering, a bathroom? Try it.

A poor sleeper, Barbara chose the bed closest to the window to avoid elevator and hall noises. She even tested her bed in the traditional bounce-the-springs manner. A surprise that first night that no traveler, no matter how seasoned, could have anticipated, disclosed her mattress had a huge, gaping hole toward the foot of the bed, obvious only by getting under the covers and actually lying down. Her ankles and feet sank into a vast void. The desk clerk assured us that there was nothing wrong with their brand new mattresses, but if we weren't happy, we could bring the matter up with the owner on Monday, as *Madame* was unavailable during weekends. We requested a board be placed between the mattress and the slats. That would have to wait for Monday, too.

It was clearly impossible for Barbara to sleep with her extremities dangling through a hole, and we had an idea of using the narrow wooden suitcase rack. By turning it upside down, feet in the air, we slid it sideways under the mattress. The narrow mattress was a made-to-measure fit between the rack's upside-down legs. Feeling more like naughty children than out-of-the-box thinkers, we restored it in the morning to avoid the anticipated scolding, and struggled to replace it again on Sunday night, knowing that our request would be viewed as if we were the archetypes of spoiled, demanding Americans.

On Monday, we discovered that the owner was as unavailable in person as during her physical absence over the weekend. She never looked us in the eye and appeared unable to activate even the smallest smile muscle, while saying with the believable candor of an actress in a farce that there was nothing wrong with our brand new mattress, but she agreed to send up a board if we absolutely insisted. True to her word, the board was there when we returned at the end of an exhausting day, mellowed by a superb multi-course dinner including *fois gras* and a bottle of good wine.

A huge jagged portion of a cast-off heavy wooden door was left propped in our room, a difficult feat in itself, because beds, a long window, the bathroom, and two suitcases took up most of the wall space our almost eight-by-ten room and bath. The scant floor space was reduced even more by the monstrously thick slab of wood resting between a wall and the bed at just enough angle to prevent it from toppling backwards onto the mattress. It was unsuitably thick and heavy for us to lift and place it over the bed slats, which wouldn't have tolerated the weight, anyhow. This meant another night of juggling with an upside-down luggage rack.

We did discover an unexpected luxury – a wall safe for money and passports. The difficulty lay in operating it. Located on the inside wall of the armoire, it read, "Instructions are on the inside of the safe door," but the door operated in such a fashion that it allowed only a slight four inch opening. The instructions were beyond view to anyone lacking holographic vision. Calling the desk clerk – yes, the phone functioned – we requested verbal instructions about how to operate the safe. His attitude again made it clear that we were annoying Americans, unable to do the simplest tasks unaided. After we insisted he show us, only then did he admit to not knowing the "simple" procedure either. He was still too young and inexperienced to have mastered the Madame's art of intimidation. We'd have to wait for help till – you guessed it – Tuesday.

When Tuesday night arrived, we had already decided to leave the hotel. We didn't want to shorten our stay in Paris, but unfortunately the other hotels we called could not assure more than a single night's reservation. They were fully booked. We hoped that Provence might be a place where tourists like us were not as plentiful as fleas and just as impossible to tolerate. But the most urgent reason for leaving Paris before we'd planned was the unresolved mattress problem.

After repacking, we checked under the beds to make sure we hadn't left anything. There, to our surprise, was a trundle bed under my bed, which Madame had the audacity to say was stored there only for a third room guest, if needed.

Onward to the charming walled city of Avignon, from where we planned to take several day trips before celebrating Christmas.

Our hotel was wonderful, as was the staff. They appreciated our speaking French; Barbara was fluent but my facility lay far at the other end of the spectrum. Nevertheless they neither scoffed nor mocked, as *Madame* had done.

I continued to relish *fois gras* every night as I promised myself to do in France. Five days before Christmas I had a heart attack. Too much cholesterol? I bless the French system of medicine and the obvious caring and expertise of the local hospital and staff.

Within minutes of my having fainted in our room, a doctor arrived with a nurse and three members of the fire department. The firefighters carried me down five flights of stairs because my stretcher wouldn't fit horizontally in the elevator. But they got me to the hospital, Barbara told me, wasting no time. I was assigned to a doctor who, himself, performed all the necessary tests and also prescribed my medications. It was amazing how quickly I learned to communicate in French. He stayed right with me in the emergency room until the next morning when I was transferred to a large room with several other patients. I spent four days in the ward before being dismissed. Barbara was there during visiting hours; when not with me, she made the rounds of small museums and galleries.

The day before my release, she was in the Pope's palace and struck up an acquaintance with a local woman, who was there with her young son. The woman and Barbara discovered they were both were painters. When Madame Gautier learned that Barbara would be in Avignon for Christmas, she insisted that my friend join their traditional extended family Christmas dinner. Barbara declined, citing my condition, but the woman absolutely insisted that I come, too. Wouldn't hear of a refusal, saying that her two brothers, one from Paris and the other from Normandy, were also going to be there. And they both were doctors, so in any emergency, I would be in good hands. Anyhow, she insisted, what more fitting a way for her family to celebrate the day than to include both of us in their family, especially since we were far from ours. Sort of like making room for us at the inn.

The *Gautier's* warmth and generosity created an indelible kaleidoscope of memories for us to attach to those of our student days from a half-century ago. An unforgettable Christmas in France.

About the Author

Claire is a world traveler and a true believer in the magic within all human beings. A teacher by profession, a gifted writer, and a woman of grace and good taste, she is seeking representation for her YA novel titled, "Then You Can See the Sky" and completing the work on a compelling Civil War novel.

She is a member of the Florida Writers Association and resides in St. Augustine Beach, Florida. Claire can be contacted by email at cmsloan3@yahoo.com.

Santa's Helper

Skye Taylor

The little girl climbed up into Santa's lap and carefully smoothed her skirt over her knees.

"I know you aren't really Santa Claus," she whispered into Santa's ear.

Lt. James "Mac" MacAlister leaned back and peered down at the girl from under the bushy white eyebrows someone had stuck on over his own sandy brows. This was not an accusation he'd been prepared for when he signed on to do this gig with the Toys for Tots program.

Mac gave the thin young shoulders a hug and confided, "I'm one of Santa's elves. Santa Claus can't be everywhere at once and right now he's busy at the North Pole. So he sent me to find out what all the good boys and girls wanted him to put on his list."

"Is that why your suit doesn't fit so well?"

"What gave me away?" He chuckled in his best Santa imitation.

"Your lap kinda feels like my daddy's used to," she said parting her knees to poke at Mac's muscular, very unSanta-like thigh.

Mac wondered if her father was a fellow Marine, or perhaps just liked to work out. Either way, she made it sound as if the man was no longer with the family.

"What would you like Santa to bring you?" he asked, trying to redirect the conversation.

"I don't need anything. Not really . . ." she trailed off wistfully. "But my brother wants one of these." She pulled a tattered page from a toy catalog out of her pocket and spread it out for him to see. It featured a Tonka Desert Fox SUV. "He's still too little, and he doesn't understand why Daddy can't come home. And Mommy says Santa Claus isn't coming to our house this year, either."

Tears prickled unexpectedly in Mac's eyes. He blinked them away and gave the little girl another hug. "Surely there must be something you would like?"

The girl folded the page from the catalog and pressed it into Mac's hand. "Just the truck for Sammy. Even Santa Claus can't bring my daddy back in time for my dance recital, and that's all I wanted. Except maybe—" she paused, then added in a hurried, hushed little voice, "maybe a new pair of ballet shoes."

Mac produced two Tootsie Pops from his voluminous pocket. "One for you and one for your brother. And I'll be sure that Santa Claus gets your message, but I need to know your name so he'll be sure to deliver the truck to the right house."

"It's Maggie," the girl chirped as she slid off Mac's lap. "Maggie Reynolds."

*****

The Desert Fox SUV was easy. Finding out where Maggie Reynolds lived wasn't hard either. Discovering the whereabouts and status of Maggie's father was the challenge. But Mac wasn't in Intelligence for nothing.

It turned out that Sergeant Don Reynolds was stationed in the Middle East, seven months into a year-long tour. His wife was pregnant with their third child who was due in less than a month, and money was tight.

Mac did some more recon to discover what Maggie's mother needed most in the way of assistance. He sent his own Marine elf, aka Sergeant Trisha Burke, out to find the SUV for Sammy and a new car seat for the coming infant. He got another buddy to promise a total overhaul of the family's aging vehicle and paid a local nursery to deliver a tree to the Reynolds home. Toys for Tots would put a few things under the tree, but there was one other surprise Mac had in the works. He hoped he could pull it off. Perhaps he could change Maggie's mind about the scope of Santa's powers.

*****

Maggie hurried to her spot. She fluffed the spangled tutu and peered over the ruffles to gaze yet again at the brand new ballet shoes that had appeared on her doorstep just that morning. They were exactly the right size, and they had ribbons that matched her tutu perfectly. How had Santa Claus known?

If only Daddy could have seen her dance tonight, then her Christmas would have been the best ever.

As the curtains began to part, the music started. Maggie quickly placed her feet in the correct position and raised her arms into an arch above her head. She lifted her chin, determined to smile and pretend that Daddy was sitting in the front row like he'd promised. The curtains parted, and she pointed her toe to begin the dance.

Then she hesitated. Her heart thumped in her chest, and tears slipped down her cheeks. There, in the front row, holding Mommy's hand sat a Marine in his best blue uniform clutching an enormous bouquet of pink roses.

Santa Claus had brought Daddy home in time after all.

About the Author

Skye Taylor lives in St. Augustine, Florida, enjoying the history of America's oldest city and taking long walks along its beautiful beaches. She posts a weekly blog, volunteers with the USO, and is currently working on book four in her Tide's Way series, a time-travel romance, and a mystery novella. Her published works include: *Whatever it Takes, Falling for Zoe, Loving Meg, Trusting Will* and non-fiction essays of her experiences in the Peace Corps.

How Christmas Became "X mas"
(An Adult Fairy Tale)
Marie Vernon

Once upon a time (for all fairy tales must begin thus), there was a small planet that whirled through the infinity of space, circling one particular star out of the millions in its galaxy. The planet's orbit caused it to return to the place from which it started in exactly 364.256363004 days. One of those three hundred and sixty-five days (for the sake of our story we'll omit the .256363004)—the most solemn, sacred and joyous day of all—the inhabitants of the small planet called *CHRISTMAS*. Yes, it was always written like that, with italicized capital letters, and the very name of the day was spoken in hushed and reverent tones.

For this Day of Days had been set aside in order that the inhabitants of the small planet (which we shall henceforth call Earth) might celebrate the birth of a particular child who was born quite humbly, but miraculously (as, indeed all Earth's children are born). The child was a boy as had long been predicted by Wise Men and the birth took place in a rough manger in an insignificant little town called Bethlehem. The birth aroused great excitement because the Wise Men had foretold that the child would become a great Teacher, sent to guide Earth's inhabitants who were, it must be admitted, becoming a bit spoiled and selfish. A flood some centuries earlier had curtailed their bad behavior for a time, but its effects had diminished, and they had sunk back into the old, evil ways. (It might be speculated that the .256363004 delay in the planet's orbit had caused that negative behavior, although this was never proven.)

For thirty-three years, the child—now a great Teacher—lived to spread his message of Peace, Love and Hope to all those who would listen. His words, however, infuriated some who feared losing their power if ever earth's inhabitants truly accepted the message He brought. To avoid this calamity, the all-powerful ones (was it mere coincidence that they also controlled the planet's wealth?) reviled the Great Teacher and all those who believed and practiced His message. They whispered that His true intent was to overthrow their rule, to take over the entire planet, to destroy all that they held dear (which included, of course, their wealth). In the end, the teacher was condemned to death.

"There!" the all-powerful ones said, "that will do it!"

How wrong they were—so great and wise a Teacher He was—that even hundreds and thousands of years after he was gone, the day of His coming was still celebrated in every corner of that small planet as the most Holy of Holidays.

Picture, if you can, a day filled with joy so sweet and solemn that the people of the small planet flocked to their churches and poured out their happiness in the beautiful words of "Silent Night" and "Adeste Fidelis." Imagine, too, hearts so overflowing with thankfulness for the gift of the Child who had been bestowed upon them that they, in turn, bestowed gifts and treasures on those they loved. On that day, the door of every home was opened to friends and strangers alike. There were fine meals prepared and much laughter and jolly games (for I have said, have I not, that *CHRISTMAS* was a joyous holiday). But always and ever they knew whose birthday it was that they celebrated, and respect and adoration for Him was foremost in every heart.

But then (and who can tell where such things begin or where they will end), the Earth people began to consider themselves very wise and wonderful indeed, for they had discovered a few (but only a few) of the universe's many secrets. They had learned to travel over their little planet at great speeds and even to rise a short distance into the vast reaches of the universe. They learned (and a great misfortune it was) how to produce weapons with which to destroy each other. They even managed to invent some weapons so mighty they were capable of blowing their entire little planet to bits, although it must be said that no one was able to explain the advantage of such an achievement.

Earth's people grew careless, too, and indifferent to the beauty of their lovely little planet. They allowed the air above them to become foul and the once-sparkling streams and rivers to turn brown with waste from their endeavors. Many of the beasts who shared the planet were hunted to extinction or their habitats destroyed.

Soon these very wise people began to lose interest in the birthday of the child, for they were busy—very, very busy—thinking of new and better ways to destroy themselves and their planet. Many of them quite forgot just what it was that was being celebrated and the very name of His day was shortened to XMAS (which saved a great deal of time for being even busier). Some remembered that the day had something to do with the exchange of gifts and the weeks before XMAS became a time of frantic buying and selling and much rushing about which made the inhabitants of Earth feel very, very virtuous, for they dearly loved to rush about. Besides, it was good for The Economy.

The Earth people took great pleasure, too, in exchanging clever and expensive greeting cards bearing pictures of their new homes and new yachts with "Happy Holly-daze" and "Have a Cool Yule" written on the inside. It was also remembered that eating and drinking had been a part of the celebration, so many indulged in wild orgies knows as Office Parties to prove that they were aware of the day's significance.

Many of them, it is true, sought to preserve the true meaning of the Most Holy of Days, but each year their numbers dwindled and each year it became easier and easier to forget that XMAS had once been *CHRISTMAS*.

And so, as all tales must, this tale of the planet Earth and her wise-foolish people must close. Although fairy tales should end happily, we can only watch and wait and hope, as the shepherds waited upon a hillside above Bethlehem two thousand years ago. Perhaps another miracle will occur, and once again, as the little planet spins through space, the universe will thrill to the sweet, reverent strains of "Adeste Fideles. . . O, come all ye faithful."

About the Author

Marie Vernon is author or co-author of published works that include regional histories SPEAKING OF OUR PAST and THE GARRISON CHURCH; the novel GRACELAND EXPRESS; true crime books DEADLY LUST and DEADLY CHARM; and mystery novels ABOVE THE FOLD and DEADLY LISTINGS. An award winning short story writer and poet, her articles, columns and book reviews have appeared in numerous publications.

The Kitty in the Basement: A Christmas Tale

Christine W. Kulikowski

Twice she tried to dodge around me, the little black cat, when I opened the front door for mail and groceries. Third time was lucky: My five-year-old daughter Dylan leaped from the school bus, scooped up the cat, and slipped around me into the house.

"Poor little Kitty, Kitty," she crooned as she nuzzled and kissed it.

"It's Susie's cat," I said. Two weeks to Christmas and I had more than enough on my to-do list. *No more problems till after Christmas, please.*

"No, it's not Susie's, Mommy. Hers is white with lots of black. This one's all black except for her tippy toes."

I took the docile creature into my arms. Guilt rushed over me. As the cat purred and kneaded my shirt I felt the bones of her back and ribs. Her skin hung loosely. She was starving and dehydrated. I hadn't seen any posters for lost cats. I made quick calls to local shelters and police stations. No lost cats reported.

"Hmm. If we have to keep her for a while, let's get her to the vet."

Dr. Gimble told us the kitty was about ten years old, judging by her eyes. But, she added, her teeth were gorgeous, those of a young cat. Someone had cared for her very lovingly to clean her teeth so often. The vet gave her booster shots for everything and kept her overnight for worming. Next day Kitty, as we were calling her now, greeted us as lost family members. She clung to Dylan's jacket.

That evening my husband Bill returned home after a care-tending weekend with his ninety-year-old mother. He gave me a "later" shrug and turned to Dylan.

"Oh no!" he gave a shout of feigned horror when he saw the cat. "We can't keep another four legs in this house! And what about the dogs?" We had four. That made sixteen legs to feed already.

"I'll find her a good home, Bill." But I knew he knew that older cats over-filled the shelters. Kittens were the big draw at Christmas. "I'll do it right after Christmas."

"But we can keep her after Christmas," Dylan insisted. "We *need* a cat." She turned to go to the basement where we had set up Kitty's quarters. The basement is warm and bright, with lots of fleecy throws everywhere, but Dylan's eyes filled with tears at the thought of Kitty all alone. Time for an executive decision.

"Okay, you can play and read in the basement to keep Kitty company. You can give her food and water and wash the bowls every day. Her litter box is in the corner. It must be clean with lots of fresh litter. Remember, basement rules."

"Yes, Mommy."

School was closed for the holidays. I didn't think Dylan would keep Kitty's quarters in order and spend time without a TV or even a phone. She could take a book, writing pad, and pencils: Basement rules.

"Don't let the dogs down." I couldn't face testing the dogs' cat tolerance. That was for after Christmas.

To my surprise Dylan spent all her time with Kitty. I

did draw the line at sleeping in the basement.

*****

Three days to Christmas. I needed to bake cookies. Bill came into the kitchen, took my arms, and lowered them.

"Listen. We need to talk." Uh-oh. That was my usual line.

"Now?"

"Now. My mother needs someone around her. She's tripping over her own feet."

I pictured the "Help, I can't get up!" lady in the commercial. "Didn't she like the emergency alert bracelet?"

"She threw the whole set-up into the garden. I hope we can get our money back."

"Did you mention that great assisted-living home you showed her?"

"She shouted in the lobby then and she shouted the same thing yesterday: 'I would rather cut my throat than go there.' "

His British mother still had her black sense of humor.

"Well—don't explode," he continued, "but remember when we talked about having Granny live with us?"

I did. I wasn't any happier about it now. More work.

"C'mon. I could live with two more legs in the house," he said with a wink.

I didn't laugh. "We'll see. Let's talk after Christmas. I can't think now."

"I know. After Christmas."

*****

Suddenly it was Christmas Eve. Where did all that time go? Decorating mindlessly and automatically humming carols, I kept thinking of Kitty and Granny. Dylan would pop upstairs to eat and talk, but mostly stayed with Kitty in the basement. I wished she wasn't so attached.

We began the holiday traditionally with a Polish Vigil on Christmas Eve. Dylan watched for the first star. Then we ate a fish dinner. After the Midnight Mass, Dylan could open her presents. Granny insisted on going to church. She was very unsteady and nearly fell on the uneven pavement, but we got her safely to the car. Bill was right. She really did need help.

After two hours of standing, kneeling, and singing Polish and English carols, Dylan should have been exhausted. She wasn't. I was. We started to open gifts, but Dylan suddenly ran out of the room.

"Wait a minute—I forgot a present." I wondered if she had been making gifts for others during the long hours of cat sitting. She tip-toed back into the room and showed her gift: a plump Kitty with a yellow bow on her head. Granny's favorite color. Kitty's long coat was stunning. It reflected red and green as the tree lights blinked on and off. Her little paws were snow white. She was purring loudly, like an old man snoring.

"Kitty is for you, Granny. She likes to sleep a lot, just like you." Granny's eyes widened. Her face glowed. She had always loved cats. She hugged Kitty. A tear ran down her cheek.

"Dylan, I told you we would decide where Kitty goes after Christmas."

"It *is* after Christmas, Mommy. You said Jesus is born at Midnight Mass."

I had.

"Then it's after Christmas, right?"

I didn't have enough words to explain to a five-year-old how time is measured.

Granny's slight voice barely reached our ears. Her face had sagged. Her joy was gone. Wistfully Granny kissed Kitty's head.

"I can't take care of a cat anymore."

"I can." Dylan spun in circles to relieve her excitement. "Daddy was saying you're moving in with us! I heard him. Mommy said after Christmas. That's today." She gazed adoringly at her father. "Just like Mary and Joseph found a home—I mean, it was a cave. But a home, too."

Galloping paws rushed in to join the party.

"The dogs, the dogs," I choked out.

Bill gave me a sideways look. Then he sent a sheepish grin. "It's fine. We kind of trained them."

"Daddy always forgets to close the basement door. So all the dogs came to see Kitty. She went *hissssss*. Bella licked her head. Sabie and Chippy ran upstairs to hide. And Joy ate all the food." Dylan giggled. "Good dogs! That's *your* present, Mommy."

I smiled at my child, my husband, and my mother-in-law.

"Of course, Granny will stay with us."

Since Bill accepted four-legged Kitty, I accepted two-legged Granny. She had been a priceless help to us as we struggled to work and care for Dylan. Granny always came in a heartbeat to stay with her; she cooked, washed laundry, cleaned house . . . I owed her at least that much.

"Ahem." I raised a glass of grape juice. "God bless us everyone! Let's thank God for six more legs to love."

About the Author

Christine Kulikowski has worked as a lab technician, actress, animal breeding and biology researcher and college instructor, grant and science writer, English literature and writing college adjunct, newspaper reporter and editor, and author of fiction. Chris' recreation has included hiking, climbing volcanoes, community theatre, dog rescue, political activism and traveling. She owns one husband, two overachieving children, two odd dogs and a cat who adopted the family last year.

Lost and Found Magic

JoannZ Gick

You never know what to expect when you go on your morning bike ride here in Florida.

It was a perfect day in Paradise, just after Thanksgiving. I noticed a brown briefcase lying on the ground, while I was riding my bike. I had to stop or hit it, as I entered my gated community. I thought about going around it, but my inner voice said "NO; it may belong to someone in the community." So I stopped and picked it up. The gold engraved initials S.C. appeared on the large tattered leather flap between the two straps.

I stopped at the clubhouse to drop off the briefcase. I entered the security code to gain access and noticed the office was open.

"Hi, Kate," I said to the secretary.

"Hi, Joanie," she replied. "What can I do for you on this beautiful morning?"

"Well, I found this leather briefcase out front; maybe it belongs to someone here."

I placed it on her desk. "Look, the initials S.C. are monogrammed on it," I pointed out.

"Okay, I'll put it on the lost and found table over by the residents' mailboxes. If it does belong to someone here, they'll see it," Kate said.

*****

I went home and shared my briefcase find with Ted. I was so excited and wanted to show it to him.

"Come on, Ted, let's go to the clubhouse for Bingo early so I can show you the leather briefcase," I begged.

"Okay, okay," Ted said in a bothered tone. He was not sharing my excitement.

Ted made an announcement after Bingo.

"Did anyone drop a leather briefcase? If you did or know someone who might have, it's at lost and found."

After Bingo, Ted and I went to look at the briefcase. Immediately, Ted saw S.C. in gold letters on the leather flap.

Ted laughed. "Yep, you are right. It certainly looks old and worn."

Ted and I picked up the leather briefcase, opened the two front buckled straps and lifted the leather flap. It was like a light was turned on, then a letter slid out onto the table.

"Oh my," I shouted, "what's happening?"

The briefcase became dark and suddenly the letter was lying in front of us. Ted picked up the letter, then began to read.

Dear Santa... Ted turned to me; we looked at each other. Ted started to read again. *...I live in Palm City, Florida. I am eight years old. My dad lost his job last year. I would like a new shirt for him. I would like a new pair of shoes for my mom and a doll for my baby sister. That would make it a perfect Christmas for me. Thank you for all the past toys you gave me. Love, Cindy*

"Ted, we must fill this wish for the little girl," I said.

All the way home, I continued talking about the letter left for Santa.

"Could the leather briefcase belong to Santa Claus?" I blurted as we turned into the driveway.

"Come on Joanie, do you really believe Santa Claus lost his briefcase out front of our community?"

"Yes, I do, Ted."

The next day, our neighbors, Sandy and Ken were in the clubhouse getting their mail when they discovered the briefcase on the lost and found table.

"Look, Ken, this briefcase looks just like the one you used when you went to your law office in New York City," Sandy said.

"Damn it, you're right," he replied.

Ken picked it up and proceeded to open the two straps. Suddenly a light glowed bright, then a letter slid out onto the table. Ken and Sandy were speechless. Ken picked up the letter then began to read:

Dear Santa,

My name is Logan. I live in Stuart, Florida. My mom is very sick. Could you please leave a new dress for my mom, a tie for me and Dad so we could look nice to go to church on Christmas to pray for mom to get better?

"What is it?" Sandy asked.

Ken and Sandy took the letter to Kate in the office and told her what just happened. Kate went with Sandy and Ken back to the lost and found table, Kate opened the briefcase ... nothing happened.

No lights. No letter. Kate laughed, "Oh, I would not have time for this. I have kids of my own to buy for."

So, Sandy locked the briefcase and placed it back on the table. Ken and Sandy took the Santa letter home, knowing they must grant the child's wish.

*****

A few days passed and the leather briefcase remained

on the lost and found table.

Justine had just finished exercise class when she decided to check her mailbox; there she noticed the leather case. She picked it up, unbuckled the straps. Suddenly the light appeared, a letter slid out onto the table in front of her. Justine took a step back and watched before picking up the letter. Then she began to read it.

Dear Santa,

My name is Emily. I live in Jensen Beach, Florida. I am very sad this Christmas. My daddy went to heaven. He was in Afghanistan and never came home. My mommy is so sad. Christmas will be very sad for her. Please bring my mom a locket so she could put dad's picture in it. I would like a Barbie doll. Please make her happy again, Santa. Thank you – Emily

Justine closed the case and brought the letter to my house. She rang my door bell. I opened the door and invited her in.

"Joanie, guess what just happened to me at lost and found? I have a letter for Santa," Justine said with concern.

"Yes, I understand," I replied.

I opened the desk drawer, removed the letter and handed it to Justine. "We have a Santa letter also."

"What should we do now?" Justine asked with a puzzled look.

*****

The next week at Bingo, Ted made another announcement. "How many of you have received a letter from the brown leather briefcase?"

A few people raised their hands–about eight.

"Let's discuss it after Bingo," Ted said.

Ken said, "When Kate opened the briefcase, nothing happened."

"We must be the chosen ones," Ted chuckled.

"I think the magic of the briefcase knows who will fill the wishes of the children for Santa Claus," I said.

"Yes, you're right," Justine replied. "So what and how can we do it?

Ted suggested, "Maybe we should bring the requested gifts to the clubhouse on Christmas Eve. I'll write a letter to Santa, place it in the briefcase, telling him where the gifts are for the children."

"Great idea," Sandy yelled out.

*****

The next few days we shopped and wrapped all the gifts. It filled all of us with great Christmas joy, being helpful elves for Santa. We all hoped Santa would get our letter.

Ted checked the brown leather briefcase daily, our letter was still there. When Ted checked Christmas Eve morning, it was gone. Ted was so excited; he called all the letter holders and told them to bring the gifts to the clubhouse.

We set our beautifully wrapped gifts in the lobby near the lost and found table surrounding the brown leather briefcase, with visions that Santa would soon appear to pick them up.

*****

Early Christmas morning, Ted and Ken went to check the clubhouse. The alarm was magically off. Ted entered hoping all was safe. Suddenly he saw **MERRY CHRIST-MAS** balloons floating in the air over the lost and found table. The gifts and the brown leather briefcase were gone. A note was where the briefcase had laid.

Ted read it out loud:

Thank you for being great helpers to make wishes come true at Christmas. Joanie, a special thank you for finding my briefcase and sharing the letters with your

friends. *Merry Christmas and a Happy New Year to all.*
   Santa
   Also on the table were bottles of champagne with big
red bows and our names attached. We adjourned, despite the early hour, to the clubhouse library to celebrate
the magic and gift of Christmas.
   Helping to supply such simple and sincere things for
others had restored the Christmas magic to each of our
lives.
   "Merry Christmas," we toasted.

About the Author

   Joann and husband Ted are busy travelers with
homes in both in New Jersey and Florida. She's a member of Sisters in Crime Central Jersey and is published
in *Crime Scene NJ 3*, and *Snowbird Christmas Volume
1*. Writing has always been a hobby and, with encourage-
ment, finds it now to be an adventure she enjoys almost
as much as traveling.

NOVELETTES

The Christmas Promise

Bruce Ann Ferguson

Melissa Andrews pulled her car into the garage, thankful the garage door opener worked. It was snowing and the temperature hovered around twenty-five degrees. Her shoulders ached from driving with so much stress—mental and emotional. The back roads had been covered in snow for several miles and now, ice formed on top of the snow. She felt lucky to have made it to the cabin without a catastrophe.

She sat behind the wheel of the car to rest for a moment. The trip from Florida had been a major headache and she had never felt so alone. *I better get the house heat started. It'll be dark soon and if the power goes out, I'll be in trouble.*

As she entered the kitchen, everything was as she had left it two years ago. The old vacation house was heated by electric baseboard heat which was turned down to fifty degrees during the winter months. Dust covered the kitchen counters, but it would be livable until she could clean. Hurriedly, she turned on all the electric heaters, hoping for quick relief from the freezing cold.

On the gas stove sat her favorite red tea kettle. It reminded her that she needed to go out to the boathouse and turn on the electric pump so lake water would be available for the toilet and shower. Purposefully, she trudged back out into the snow and made her way to the boathouse. Once she pushed snow out of the way and opened the old door, she turned on the lights and tried to find the right switch to turn on the pump. After a couple of tries, she was rewarded with the sound of machinery. She looked over at the yellow motor boat then dashed back to the warmth of the house.

She put away the few groceries she had purchased at the Quik Stop and prepared a cup of tea to warm her.

The dining room table looked inviting. She had spent many happy days there during the summers when her children were young. She sat down, still in her coat, and drank the hot tea as the cup also warmed her hands.

The dining room was part of an L-shaped great room. Both the living room and dining room were enclosed with large crank-out windows allowing a full view of the trees and the lake beyond. The cottage sat at the tip of a peninsula and was surrounded on three sides by water. Today, the view was beautiful. Snow crystals covered every twig and tree branch, while the rhododendron leaves received the weight of the snow with grudging acceptance.

The house had been in her husband David's family for fifty years. It sat on top of a low mountain in the northwest New Jersey Lake District only a two hour drive from Manhattan. The nearest main road was two miles from the cottage.

Melissa sat in the solitude and listened for the usual sound of lapping water, but she heard nothing. The lake was frozen and quiet. Perhaps it was in hibernation after the busy summer activities ended, she thought.

Soon, a lone deer appeared next to the window and tried to eat the frozen rhododendron leaves. When the leaves refused to be eaten, the deer scampered away leaving footprints in the snow. *It's odd, how nature survives in conditions we cannot tolerate*. She wondered where the deer would find its dinner.

For a long time Melissa sat staring out at the snow flurries and tried not to think. The winter storm raged outside the window; Mother Nature was as angry as *she* was.

Melissa's life had not turned out as she had planned. Here she sat, sixty years old and alone. She had left her husband David in Florida. Her children were grown and married. She laughed harshly. Even her grandchildren were self-sufficient. No one needed her and knowing that made her sad. She was like an abandoned suitcase after the vacation... vastly important during the trip, but now in the way.

When Melissa felt the house warming, she went upstairs to make the bed in the master bedroom. The room had a lovely view out across the lake with its vaulted ceiling and French windows. The room was painted off-white and decorated in periwinkle blue, her favorite color. The old furniture was now painted white. She treasured the white antique iron bed. Melissa dragged out the blankets and comforter from plastic bags and made the bed for one person.

When she was finished, she decided to snuggle under the covers and take a nap; she could eat later. Many hours later, Melissa woke in the middle of the night totally disoriented. For a moment, she was confused about where she was; then she remembered.

Across the snowy lake she could see lights on at the gatekeeper's house. Comforted that she was not alone, she turned over and went back to sleep to the sounds of howling wind.

Melissa woke slowly; *what time is it?* The sun was reflecting off the icy lake so it had to be at least eight o'clock in the morning. She wondered if the roads were open, not that she planned to go anywhere. She just needed to know she wasn't trapped.

Her cottage had no television reception, so she turned on the small radio which sat on the bedside table. The news was all about the snowstorm and how it would hamper schools from opening and Christmas shoppers from getting to the many shopping centers at the base of the mountain. *I'm snowbound, I guess.*

She got up quickly and wrapped herself in the old robe she kept hanging on the back of the bedroom door. The electric had apparently stayed on, so the cottage was warm. She went downstairs and looked out across the lake, awed by its beauty. It looked like a Currier & Ives Christmas card.

Then she went to the old black telephone and lifted the receiver and was amazed to hear a dial tone. She breathed a sigh of relief because her cell phone often had little to no reception there.

After a breakfast of coffee and toast with jam, the telephone rang. Melissa jumped, her heart rate picking up. She wasn't ready to answer any questions. Although there was no caller ID on the telephone, she guessed it might be Mike, the lake caretaker, checking on her. Her arrival would not have gone unnoticed, another comforting thought. She picked up the telephone.

"Are you okay over there?" Mike asked. "I wanted to be sure you were able to negotiate the road through the woods. I plowed it a day ago, but you know how it gets."

"I'm fine," she said.

"How long do you expect to be there?"

"I'm not sure, maybe through Christmas."

"Do you need firewood?"

"Yes, thank you, whenever you have time."

"I'll be over this afternoon and load some in your laundry room to keep it dry. If you need me to, I'll start the fireplace for you. How about the water pump, did you get it going?"

"Yes, I think it's okay, but if you could check it when you bring the wood. I'd really appreciate it."

"Okay, I'll see you later."

Just as she hung up the phone, it rang again. Melissa answered without thinking to find it was her daughter, Sherry.

"Mom, what in the name of heaven are you doing at the lake house in the middle of December?" she asked. "We've been worried sick. Dad called and said you left home and he wasn't sure where you were."

"Did he mention the fight we had?" I asked.

"No, he didn't say anything about that, but he seemed worried about your safety and suggested I give you a call at the lake house. Honestly, Mom, aren't you a little too old for this sort of drama? I know Dad has been a creep over the years, but why leave now?"

"I'm just fine. And I'm not ready to talk about it, thank you. The cottage is in good condition, the heat is on and the gas stove is functioning. I picked up a few groceries and just talked with Mike Malone, so I'm not alone up here. I'm okay."

"But Mom—"

Melissa felt her temper brewing. "Sherry, I need time to think. My life span is shrinking and I need to think about where and how I want to spend those years. I've decided to stay here through the Christmas holidays and enjoy the solitude."

Her daughter sighed as though she was exasperated. "Well, I think you should come home. Dad needs you. I can't take care of him. You know how demanding he is. After all, I have a family of my own to care for."

Before Sherry could go on and on, Melissa decided to end the conversation. "The tea kettle is boiling over, honey. I'll talk to you later."

Melissa sat down on the old red sofa with a cup of tea and rethought the last week. *Well, here I am. After thirty-five years of marriage, I've left my husband. Did he cheat on me all of those years? Or, maybe just since I've grown old. I often wondered. Maybe, I didn't want to know the truth. Maybe I didn't care. Maybe I knew, but wasn't ready to do anything about it.*

He was a good provider and I had my children and friends to fill the voids when he was busy. It's probably my fault that he found someone else...I'm too dependent and boring. I'm like an old slipper, comfortable and dependable.

Tears trickled down her cheek. All the years of cleaning house and cooking meals now felt like wasted efforts. *How did I go wrong? I believed we were a team. We were supposed to grow old together; him loving me and being appreciative of my efforts. What happened? I always thought we would walk off into the sunset holding hands. Not this, him holding some twenty-five year old's hand and me alone.*

*****

Melissa looked out across the snowy lake and remembered three nights ago when she had seen David out to dinner with one of his female employees. They were holding hands just as David had held hers when they were courting.

He hadn't seen Melissa. He thought she was out to a play with friends, but at the last minute, Melissa had felt ill and decided to skip the night out with the girls. When she'd begun to feel better, she decided to go to her favorite Italian restaurant alone. It was there she saw David with Patricia Copley.

Melissa was frozen in her seat as she watched David preening in front of the young girl. The girl was laughing at his comments and the looks they exchanged told Melissa they were sleeping together. David kept pushing his hair away from his face like a goofy movie star. After watching them for several minutes, Melissa felt like she was going to throw up so she left the restaurant and ran for home.

As she entered her kitchen she screamed profanities and in a fury, broke several dishes. Eventually, her anger spent, she calmed down and got a glass of wine. Then she sat down in the living room to wait for David.

Hours later he came home looking a little worn out. His face was flushed from sex and he smelled of perfume. When he saw her sitting in the living room, he tried to hurry past her to the bedroom.

"David, come sit down," she said. "We need to talk." He stood like a statute in the doorway. She continued. "Tonight, I went to Luigi's Italian Restaurant and saw you there holding hands with Patricia Copley. She's younger than your daughter—have you lost your mind?"

David looked defensive. "So what? You're not interested in me. You're always busy with your friends. What do you expect me to do...wait in line?"

She remembered the white hot rage that almost choked her. "I don't *expect* you to do anything, but don't blame *me* for your adultery. You're a grown man and can do whatever you want, but you aren't going to see other women while you're married to me.

"Over the years, when you were aloof for a period of time, I blamed myself for not giving you enough attention. Now I see that I was wrong about that. You were cheating and feeling guilty, that's why you were aloof.

"Taking Patricia Copley to a restaurant where we are well known humiliates *me*. The fact that she is in her twenties makes us both look like fools. I deserve an explanation."

He shrugged. "I'm sorry you saw me."

She stared at him. Surely he had more to say than that? But he didn't make any further excuses or offer any explanation.

"There have been others, right, David?" she asked, washing down the words with a long sip of wine.

"A few, over the years. But what does it matter? That's in the past."

"I see," she'd said, though she didn't. "Why?"

"I don't know, Melissa."

His voice had been emotionless. It was as if he was discussing the weather. She'd been so surprised by his lack of reaction, she didn't know what to do or say. He simply sat quietly staring at the floor.

"You may choose not to discuss this with me, but I am furious with you and your childish behavior. This is *not* going away."

Then, she rose from the sofa, went up to their bedroom and locked the door. David slept in the guest room that night and she stayed in their room until he left for work. When she heard the door close, she went downstairs, got a cup of coffee and thought about the previous evening.

His words ricocheted around in her mind infuriating her. *"I'm sorry you saw me...."*

Then she remembered his body language. He sat slouched in a chair, anxious to get away from her, totally disinterested in what she said. She'd been boring him, she suddenly realized.

I won't bore him anymore. For years, she'd made excuses in order to stay married to a man she now saw was a self-centered pig. *No more.* She went upstairs in a state of fury and packed two suitcases. When finished, she threw in pictures of her kids and grandkids and drove away. She didn't even glance in the rear view mirror.

During the three-day drive to the lake house, she'd cried and battled with herself. After all these years, how could David care so little about their relationship? Didn't she mean anything to him?

How could he embarrass me and our grown children by openly dating another woman? Then there was the age issue. Did he expect her to stay married to him while he was sleeping with another woman.....especially a woman younger than their daughter? Melissa couldn't let herself imagine David in bed with this child...it was too painful to comprehend. *What can I do?*

Those were questions without answers. Finally, after analyzing the situation from every angle possible, she decided to stop thinking about David and just drive. Oddly enough, just driving, eating and sleeping soothed her anguish and restored some energy.

*****

Now it was mid-morning and Melissa decided to listen to the radio and clean the house. The house looked as neglected as she felt. As she cleaned, her thoughts returned to David.

He's probably glad for the break; glad that someone finally had the guts to end the charade. Oh, he'll tell the kids how worried he is about me and he doesn't know why I left, but deep down he'll be happy to be free. He can go out with Patricia Copley any time he wants without encountering an angry wife at home.

By mid-afternoon, the cottage sparkled and the pictures of the kids were placed so Melissa could see them from both the sofa and her bed. She liked to look at the grandchildren's faces. They were so innocent and full of life.

Christmas was near and she would miss seeing them this year. Tears sprang to her eyes and as she wiped them away she saw a deer peering at her through the window. It had been watching her....she didn't know how long, but the very presence of the magnificent animal calmed her jagged heart.

She decided to stop thinking and reread her favorite novel. Each year, she read the same book during the Christmas holidays and each year, she found a new aspect of the book to enjoy.

Melissa got a cup of hot chocolate and settled on the

sofa nested in her comforter surrounded by the outside snow. As she began the book, she could hear the wind blowing through the trees. She was at peace at last.

The next morning, as Melissa finished cleaning the upstairs level of the house, she heard someone knock on the door. It was her friend from across the lake, Judy O'Conner.

"Wow!" Judy exclaimed "I didn't expect to see you here in this snowstorm! Where's David?"

"He's not with me. He's in Florida. I decided I needed some time alone."

"I can't believe, after all these years, you finally left that bastard." Judy laughed. "No one could deserve it more than David."

"Do you really think that?" Melissa asked, taken aback. "I thought you loved David. You always laughed at his jokes and seemed interested in what he had to say. I thought everyone here at the lake simply tolerated me because David married me."

"Melissa, you have my full support, but it's too late in the day to get into all the things that are wrong with David. We need considerable time for that discussion," Judy laughed. "Here, I brought you a casserole and some home baked bread." Judy hugged Melissa tightly and with a tear in her eye, said, "Stay strong....I'll be back soon."

As she closed the door, snow blew in. Then Melissa felt ashamed for talking about David behind his back. Judy left her wondering what she knew about David that Melissa did not.

Suddenly, she felt clammy and shaky; she needed to sit down. *This is terrible, not knowing if everyone else thinks I'm an idiot because of David.* Immediately, she thought of all the available women that lived at the lake and wondered if he was hitting on them or, worse yet, their daughters. *Perhaps, I was the laughing stock of the lake, with everyone knowing secrets about David....*

She went into the kitchen and poured herself a glass of wine to help calm down. When that didn't work, she lay down to calm her racing heart while terrible thoughts of dying there alone in the lake house entered her mind.

Later, when she got herself under control, she ate the casserole Judy had brought. During dinner, she read her book. Around nine o'clock, she settled down in bed with the book and eventually drifted off to sleep.

During the night, she dreamed of large waves crashing down on her and woke with her heart pounding. She'd almost drowned when a child. She'd been swimming in the ocean with her dad when a large wave turned both of them upside down. She would have drowned if her father had not grabbed her at the last minute. As an adult, she was unafraid, but respectful of the ocean's power.

But, whenever she was anxious or stressed out, the wave would return in her dreams. The wave was always mountainous with a curling top that threatened to engulf her. She couldn't outswim it, she couldn't outrun it. It was terrifying. It took her hours to get back to sleep. *I'm driving myself crazy.*

The next morning she began to think about Christmas. *A Christmas tree would brighten up the cottage while I'm wallowing in my own misery. I have no house to decorate, parties to plan or food to prepare. I'll go into town and get a tree just for myself, a small one that I can carry from the car and decorate.*

In the small town at the foot of the mountain, the snow had melted off the roads and people were out shopping for Christmas. Melissa busied herself with finding just the right tree and decorations for her solo Christmas. After spending another hour food shopping, she went into the local arts and crafts store and bought art supplies.

As a young woman, she'd thought of nothing except becoming a great landscape painter. After she met David she slowly gave up painting, even though she'd been told she had a real talent for it.

I wonder why? Perhaps I'll try to paint the beauty of the snow covered woods with the visiting deer. The view from the cottage bedroom would also make a nice landscape. She felt happier just thinking about painting again.

She went into the village bookstore and roamed happily through the stacks of books and found novels for the grandkids and her grown children. Each year, she gave them a book and she didn't want to break a tradition just because David was a loser.

After she'd finished book shopping, she noticed it was late afternoon. So she hurried back home to arrive before dusk. When she walked into the cottage, she was laden with packages and a Christmas tree. That evening, she put on Christmas music and decorated the little tree with tiny white lights and colorful Christmas balls.

When she finished, she got herself a glass of wine and sat looking at the tree, remembering the many Christmas seasons she and David had shared. She reminisced about the joys of watching their children grow and all the many bicycles and dollhouses they'd put together late at night as the children slept.

I'm blessed with good memories. Many women don't have a good life with a beautiful home and money to spend without worry. I was one of the lucky ones.

Her thoughts turned to David. She wondered what he was doing now. Was he out with Patricia? Secretly, she hoped he was shuffling around the empty house with no hot dinner or clean clothes. *Here I am sitting in a warm cottage with a Christmas tree and homemade bread.*

With that thought, she went to bed with her book and a cup of hot cocoa. The next morning, she realized she'd slept through the night without the bad dream. *Maybe I'm on the road to recovery.*

After breakfast and a shower, she planned to wrap

the books for the kids and prepare them for mailing. There was a knock on the door...it was Mike McGuire. "The phone company thinks something is wrong with your line. People have been trying to get you, but the phone seems to be out of order," he said.

"Good grief! I took it off the hook two days ago and forgot to put it back." She laughed and dashed to return the phone to operable condition. As Mike left laughing and scratching his head, the phone rang.

"What in the name of heaven are you doing up there?" her son Jason snapped. "You have Sherry and me worried to death. We've been calling you for two days." She could feel his anger, not unlike that of his father's. He continued to rage. "It could be dangerous up there in the winter. You could fall on the ice or hunters with guns could hurt you. We want you to come home. If you don't want to go to your house, you can stay with me and Sandra. Just come home.....I'm afraid for you."

Melissa listened as her grown son admonished her. He was trying her patience. He sounded like David, talking to her as if she was a child that required him to use small words. When had that happened? *Now, I'm the child?*

"Well, I'm sorry that you've been worried, but right now, I'm safe, warm and enjoying a Christmas tree which I put up all by myself. I miss you kids and the grandkids, but this separation from your father is long overdue. I don't want to discuss the reasons why I left, just let me have this Christmas alone. I need to think."

After a long pause, Jason said, "All right, if you promise to call both Sherry and me each day to let us know you're all right."

"Okay," she said. "I'll keep in touch. But you really don't need to worry. Judy O'Conner is at her cottage across the lake and Mike McGuire just left. They're checking with me daily, so I'll be fine. And I'm a big girl." She laughed, amazed at how calm and content she felt.

Melissa remembered the summer days at the lake house when Jason and Sherry were kids. They would jump from the car as soon as it was parked and run across the front dock and dive into the lake. The house was always filled with kids and she always cooked for ten people counting all the kids' friends. During the day, everyone swam or sailed the sunfish. At night the family played Trivia or Parcheesi. Those were happy times.

Now she had two adult children telling her what to do. Melissa recalled her conversation with Jason. *Perhaps the kids knew about their father long before me. Maybe they're not surprised that I left. Jason did not seem surprised and he had not asked why. He seemed only concerned about my welfare. I wonder if David asked Jason to call....*

She lit the fireplace and sat down in the ancient rocking chair next to the fire. It was warm and cozy; the Christmas tree sparkled in the corner of the living room as she closed her eyes and let her thoughts drift back in time.

****

They were married just after David graduated from college. He went to work for his father's insurance agency. The agency was financially successful and well known in the community and both David and his father were delighted that he had joined the family business.

David was determined to be successful and worked long hours under his father's guidance. As computer usage became more common in businesses, David suggested they integrate computers into their business. He tried to explain how much time and money could be saved if the company used the new invention to maintain records, payments and sales leads.

Eventually, the relationship between father and son became strained. David understood how utilization of computers could grow the business, but his dad wanted operations to remain the same. It was a difference of "old school" versus "new school" thinking.

As time progressed, the differences between the two men reached a point where David's father fired him. David was furious and vowed to get even by starting his own insurance agency and taking his dad's customers.

Then fate intervened. Before David could get his own company up and running, his father died of a heart attack. David was sick with guilt and for many years, he blamed himself for his dad's death.

She remembered sitting in this very rocker trying to console David shortly after his father passed away. They'd gone to the lake house to get away from his mother who was distraught and angry.

The whole community seemed to blame David for putting stress on his dad. Or at least, that was David's opinion. He'd wanted to "hide out" for a while. Thinking back, she remembered having very little respect for David at the time.

David was not one to deal with difficulties of his own making. It was always someone else's fault. He was a master at the blame game...twisting events so he was faultless.

He inherited his father's business and by using modern computer technology, grew the agency until it was twice the original size. During this time, their lives became very busy.

David was away from home often and worked late many nights, but Melissa never gave it any thought. She was busy raising two children, managing two homes and handling volunteer duties.

During those years, David treated her with respect and participated in the children's activities. They had a good sex life and Melissa was happy. She'd thought David was, too.

When did I become unhappy? Was it when I saw

David out with Patricia, or have I been dissatisfied for some time? Age changes things, but it wasn't only ageing, it was a subtle loss of togetherness over a long period of years.

Am I willing to grow old alone? Or have I already been alone and just didn't know it? She took a deep breath and wiped away a tear. Even thinking of how David had fooled her made it hard to breathe.

Am I willing to live alone or will I put up with a cheating husband to prevent that? Will I go back and pretend everything is okay in order to avoid making difficult changes in my life? Throughout my life, I have given big decisions a great deal of time. I need time to heal and think; then maybe I'll make the right decision.

****

Melissa went to bed and pulled the covers over her head as a child might. She hid from her own thoughts of horrible debilitating diseases she might face alone.

Early the next morning, Judy called. "Let's go to lunch and get off this damn lake! I'm bored stiff and tired of baking bread. A change is called for, along with an adult beverage," she said laughing. "Meet me at the boat landing at noon and I'll drive."

Melissa's mind raced for excuses, unsure if she was ready to discuss her situation. Then she decided to go ahead. Maybe she'd feel better after talking with Judy.

"Okay," Melissa said sarcastically, "I'll drag my body out into the snow and drive around the lake on snow covered roads to meet an old friend."

"See you at noon," Judy said laughing as she slammed down the phone.

She was always so full of life. I loved that about her. Perhaps Judy is just what I need at this moment. Melissa showered and dressed in her warmest outfit.

She called Jason and Sherry as promised and told

them about her lunch plans with Judy. They urged her to have fun and to tell Judy they said "Hello."

Then, before she could get out the door, the phone rang again. Feeling alive and happy, she picked it up without a thought.

"How are you?" David asked.

"Not good," she responded as her heartbeat raced.

"You're being ridiculous. Staying up there in the bitter cold is nuts when you could be here in Florida enjoying the warm winter."

"That much is true, but I need time to think. You know what a careful decision maker I am."

"Look, you're making too much of this. I need you to come home. The kids and grandkids want you home. Everyone is asking me why you left and I don't know what to tell them."

"Tell them the truth. That I caught you with a woman less than half your age and it made me mad. You're really good at spinning stories. Make something up or blame it on me. I really don't give a damn. I'm surprised to hear from you at all. I would have thought you'd be out with your 'young thing' at a motel celebrating. What happened, did you run out of Viagra?"

"Stop it, Melissa. The melodrama does not become you. Just get your ass home for Christmas and I'll forget all about this, okay?"

"Not okay," she said. She slammed down the telephone and dashed out into the cold to meet Judy, leaving the ringing telephone behind her.

Once she and Judy were settled into a quiet booth in their favorite restaurant, Judy began to talk.

"As you know, I've known David since we were kids. We grew up together here at the lake. He is two years older than me, but one summer when I was sixteen we dated. He was the first man I was in love with. Eventually, we made love. I was wild about him and our future together. Actually, David never talked about a future together, but after we had slept together, I stupidly assumed we would get married when we finished college."

Judy stopped talking and drank some of her wine. She thought for a few minutes before continuing. "Then I got pregnant and David dropped me like a hot potato. At first, he refused to talk to me. I kept calling him, I had no other choice. When I finally reached him to discuss what we should do, he accused me of having sex with other guys.

"He said the baby could not possibly be his because he had always used a condom when we made love. I was heartbroken. His lack of responsibility for the pregnancy shocked me.

"I was only sixteen and so stupid. I suggested we get married. I remember him laughing and saying, 'I don't want to marry you.' His response to my plea simply sucked the life out of me."

Judy sipped her wine. For several minutes she was quiet, then she continued. "After crying for a couple of weeks and still trying to contact David with no success, I decided to get an abortion. I told my mother about the pregnancy and we cried together. I never told my dad.

"My Mother paid for the abortion and went with me to the doctor. She took care of me during the weeks that followed when I was so depressed. It was a terrible time for both of us.

"David's parents never knew about the baby. They were Catholic and would have thrown a fit if they'd known about the abortion."

Judy paused to wipe tears from her eyes. Melissa sat silent. She felt blindsided by Judy's admission. Finally, Judy continued.

"To this day, I think of that little baby and wonder what it might have looked like or become. Every year on the anniversary of the abortion, I imagine what my child might be doing if it had lived."

She reached for her wine and looked over at Melissa.

"And you know what is worse? In all these years when I've seen him at the lake, David has never once asked me about the baby. He is a real creep, Melissa. You're well rid of him."

Melissa took Judy's shaking hand in hers. They both wiped tears from their eyes and when they had both regained their composure, Melissa spoke.

"I'm not shocked at his behavior, but I am surprised that he never told me this. I've seen him hide from responsibility when things go bad. I'm just sorry it I happened to you. Thank you for telling me."

"You're a better person than he is," Judy said as she wiped her eyes again.

"I was never able to have another baby. Apparently something went wrong with the abortion. I tried for years when I was married to Jack, but nothing worked. That baby, mine and David's, was my only chance at motherhood....but I didn't know it when I was sixteen. It's strange how things work out."

"Judy, I'm so sorry, but crying won't help. If it did, I wouldn't have left home after catching him with another woman. The worst part of my story is the woman was less than thirty. She looked remotely like a twenty year old version of me. Guess he likes brunettes. What she sees in him is obvious; money and prestige. He probably thinks she loves him. What an old fool he is."

Melissa looked out the window of the restaurant and watched a young mother pulling a sled loaded with a small, laughing child. They both looked so happy and Melissa felt a tug of jealousy.

The two women sat quietly for a while enjoying the warm fire and companionship. They talked about the new families at the lake and Judy's life in New York City.

Finally, Judy asked the question Melissa dreaded. "What are you going to do about David?"

Melissa sighed. "I'm not quite sure. He called just as I was leaving the house. He demanded that I return and

I hung up on him. Beyond that, I'm not sure what to do except to take a great deal of time thinking about my next step.

"Growing old has never bothered me before. But now, it gives me pause. Judy, I'm not young anymore. No one wants a sixty year old woman. We are about as desirable as the plague."

"I'm lonely," Judy said slowly. "When I first divorced Jack, it was easy to be alone. I was fifty. I felt and looked younger. Now, I feel differently. Life is hard for an older woman. Society is all about couples. Even close friends have dinner parties and I'm not invited. I'm extra baggage and too needy."

She gazed out the window for a while, then looked at Melissa with a sad smile.

"It's true. I find myself craving a sympathetic ear. I have needless conversations with clerks in stores. At times, I long for someone to come home to. I'm old and lonely.

"I have no children to visit, no grandchildren to watch grow up and no husband to share memories with. It's hard being me," Judy laughed, but her eyes gave away the truth to her statement.

"I'm sorry," Melissa whispered around the lump in her throat. "I can't imagine." *Actually, I can imagine and the picture in my mind is not a pretty one.*

After they ate a decadent dessert, Judy asked Melissa how she met David.

"I was dating someone else, a local boy named Scott Walker, who was working his way through law school. He was kind and considerate. We both thought we would marry. Then I met David.

"David was on the football team and well known on campus. He was two years older than me and my friends considered him 'a real catch'. He was in my Art History class.

"Why David ever asked me for a date is a mystery to

me. He was this big football star and I was an art major who was only moderately attractive. Then, when he pursued me and kept asking me out, I thought I'd hit the lottery.

"My social status on campus rocketed and I became known as 'David Andrews' girlfriend'. I must admit, I was flattered and began to enjoy my new position in campus society."

Melissa paused for a moment to enjoy the coffee the waiter had just poured for them. Judy said, "Keep talking, I'm really interested."

"David demanded that I date only him, so I reluctantly broke up with Scott who I thought I loved. Scott was devastated and begged me to reconsider, but David convinced me he was serious about our relationship.

"With Scott out of the picture, David took over every part of my college life. I was going where David wanted to go, socializing with his friends, tagging along to all of David's games and mostly, praising him for his great athletic ability and good looks. Now that I think back, it's clear that David was like a tornado taking me into another world and I went along joyfully.

"Did I ever really love David? I don't know, maybe I was so flattered by his attentions that I simply assumed that if he loved me, I must love him.

"Our married life was just like college....it was all about what David wanted or required. My needs were never even discussed.

"I don't know, maybe I didn't have any needs or maybe I was so busy making David's life perfect that I didn't realize I had needs of my own. Either way, I was young and stupid!

"When he gave me a gift or did something nice for me, he wanted an audience to witness him being a great and generous husband. Eventually, I came to understand that David lacked depth.

"He's like a freshwater spring that appears to be hundreds of feet deep, but is really only a few feet deep. If he isn't talking about himself, he's disinterested." Melissa laughed to herself.

"I'm boring you with all this stuff," she said to Judy.

"No you're not. I'm interested in what married life to David was like. Remember, that was what I thought I wanted."

Melissa sat back in her chair and continued. "Our life was all about him and, strangely enough, I grew not to expect anything from him. I learned how to make myself happy and how to deal with the hardships of life on my own.

"I could not expect David to hold me and console me during the difficult times. He was—is—incapable of caring for another person. Truthfully, he did not want to deal with the down sides of life like parenting, illness or aging. I guess I convinced myself that dealing with life's problems alone was easier than including David." Melissa became pensive for a moment.

"What a realization!" she said to Judy. "I just described the type of man I detest and I've been living with one for thirty-five years. I must be making some type of progress!"

They laughed loudly and toasted Melissa reaching adulthood.

As she drove along the bumpy, snow packed road, back to the cottage she felt both content and a little afraid of the future.

I've had quite a day....I've taken a giant step toward getting to know myself.

*****

The next morning, she woke to a ringing cell phone. "Hello," she said in a sleepy voice.

"Are you leaving for home today? I just looked at the weather and if you leave this morning you could be off the mountain before the next storm hits," David stated.

"No, I was not planning to leave today. Or tomorrow, either. In fact, I'm staying up here through the holidays. I'm not sure if I'm *ever* coming back to live with you. I need time to think about our marriage and your unfaithfulness."

For a few minutes David was silent. Melissa knew he was furious that she would refuse to do as he told her. Then he said, "What's to think about? I made a mistake and I apologized for it. Don't make a big deal out of this, okay?"

Melissa laughed out loud. "Your apology isn't very meaningful to me. In fact, it sucked. You hardly said a word, then you tried to blame your infidelity on me. When did I ever do anything *other* than think of you?

"Don't make me laugh, David. With both of us thinking of your needs, I can't understand why you'd need another woman." She took a deep breath and surged ahead.

"But, here's a question for you. If we're both thinking about *your* needs, who's thinking about *mine*? No one, that's who."

She could hear his controlled breathing on the phone, but he didn't say a word.

"Actually," she continued, "I've been questioning your sanity. You've always made fun of the old guys who divorce their wives of many years to marry a trophy wife. Now we're the old couple. You should be ashamed of yourself, David. I've always been a good wife to you."

She paused to see if he wished to comment, but the telephone was silent on his end.

"I want you to know, even if I decide to get a divorce, I thank you for providing such a beautiful home for me and our children. You were a good father. I thought you were a good husband and that's why this is so hard for me. I thought you loved me."

"I do love you," David said at last. "You don't understand. I don't want a divorce, just come home and we can talk."

"Like we talked the other night when you sat there like a stone and said nothing? I don't think so, David. This break has given me plenty of time for reflection and frankly, you don't measure up in the 'I care about you' department. All you care about is yourself.

"You're chasing this child around like a dog in heat. Didn't you stop to think that I might divorce you if I found out about Patricia?"

"I never thought you'd find out!" David blurted out. "I didn't mean to hurt you or our marriage."

"So, let me see if I've got this straight. It's okay for you to run around if I don't find out about it? Why do you need these young girls?"

"They make me feel young again. The young women are optimistic about life; they're so alive and unjaded. They think I'm wonderfully wise and handsome. They laugh at my corny jokes and pretend I'm brilliant. You *know* I'm not brilliant and you no longer think I'm wonderful. You've seen me at my worst and most vulnerable. It's not the same with you."

Melissa's anger ebbed. She felt sorry for David and his childlike confession. "David, all marriages age over the years. The hot sex and romance diminish over time and a quiet, caring companionship take its place. I was happy, or at least I thought I was until this happened. Now, I'm not sure I want to come back at all. What will change?"

"I promise not to run around on you ever again," he said. "Now, will you come back?"

"I honestly don't know. But I won't be back before Christmas."

"What do you want from me?" he screamed into the phone, his anger like a venom. "I said I was sorry and now I have to listen to all this crap? Women.....who can figure them out.....certainly not me! I'm sick of this conversation. I'll talk to you later." He slammed down the telephone leaving Melissa in silence.

She clicked off the cell phone and sat in the bed thinking. *He was a good father and provider. He can't help that he's self-centered. He was an only child and spoiled rotten by his parents. I'll never be of any use to him except to provide him with a reason for not marrying any of those other women.*

"Is that any kind of life for me?" she asked herself out loud. Melissa felt tears forming in her eyes when she thought of her own sagging flesh compared to that of a twenty-five year old woman. *I can't compete with that. I can imagine a life of pretending that everything is okay, one of keeping up appearances to family and friends. I don't think I can do that, either.*

She began to cry in earnest and realized she was clutching the comforter tight to her chest. *Even if I have to live alone forever, pretending to be happy might be worse. I feel sorry for David. And I feel sorry for me.*

Finally, she got up and showered. After eating a cup of yogurt and drinking a cup of coffee, she looked out the window and saw the snow covered trees in a new light. *Maybe I'll paint.*

She pulled on a pair of sweatpants and an old flannel shirt of David's. Then, she dragged out all the art supplies she'd purchased. The paint tubes felt familiar in her hands and as she placed the brushes in an old water pitcher, she began to smile.

Once the easel was in place in the dining room, she coated the white canvas with a soft wash of burnt sienna and waited for that to dry. Then, she began to sketch. After several thumbnail sketches, she nodded.

She became so engrossed in the painting that lunchtime came and went. As darkness began to fall, she looked at her watch. It was almost five in the afternoon.

She stood back from the painting and smiled. Then she got a glass of wine and stood admiring her work. The painting was *good*.

The white snow showed up against the dark wood of the trees and bushes which created a sharp contrast with the greens of the remaining leaves. The whites were not stark white, but a combination of greys and pastel colors where the light hit the snow.

A young deer reached up to eat a snow covered rhododendron leaf. The soft burnt umber of the deer's coat brought warmth and tenderness to an otherwise cold, snowy landscape. Somehow she'd captured the vulnerability of the deer as it sought food in a harsh environment.

As she ate her supper of soup and sandwich, she continued to stare at the painting. It was as if someone else had created it. *Why did I stop painting?* She didn't know the answer, but she knew she would never again give it up.

*****

The next morning when she called her children she announced that she was painting again. Both expressed surprise and delight and encouraged her to create some landscapes for their homes. After chatting a few minutes with each of them, she hung up the phone feeling young again.

Painting is bringing me back to the person I was before I met David. As she gazed at the painting in the morning light she felt like the hopeful college girl she once was. Then, she understood what had been missing in her life...painting.

To celebrate finding herself, she decided to go Christmas shopping. There was a huge mall not too far from the foot of the mountain. She'd buy herself a nice Christmas outfit, maybe.

She dressed with care, wearing her warmest black turtleneck, black slacks and chunky, silver earrings. Her short, dark hair was brushed into its stylish cut. She added a winter white coat and knee high, black leather boots. When she looked into the mirror, she was astonished at how much better she looked with a little bit of makeup. When was the last time she'd taken the time to really look at herself?

As she drove down the mountain, she thought about nothing except painting. Everywhere she looked, she could see a landscape ready to be painted. *I wish I had brought a good camera when I left Florida.*

Now and then, though, thoughts of David's unfaithfulness tugged at the corners of her mind. *Am I strong enough to get a divorce? What a mess my life is. Maybe David's right. Maybe I should drive straight back to Florida.*

Before she let herself drift off into self-pity, she took a deep breath and brought herself back to reality. *No, I'm my old self today and I want to shop and return home to the cottage and paint. I might even stay there the rest of my life, painting and sketching. Forget about David. It's all about me now. He can do whatever he wants.*

The mall was mobbed and parking was insane. Once she got inside, she got into the spirit of the season and shopped for Jason's wife Sandra, and Sherry. She bought each of them an expensive pair of earrings and lovely cashmere sweaters. Then she purchased the usual golf shirt and sweater for Jason and Doug, Sherry's husband. She arranged for Macy's to wrap and ship the gifts to Florida.

The grandkids would get Sports Authority gift certificates via Amazon, but since Melissa wanted them to have something to open, she bought each of them silly pajamas in various designs and had the pajamas shipped. All the gifts would arrive after Christmas, but they would be welcome regardless of the timing.

She treated herself to a red cashmere turtleneck,

black slacks, earrings and various other things which she could not live without. Then, she went to the bookstore and bought three new bestsellers.

Carrying all the bags became quite a chore. She decided to take a break and soon found a coffee shop which had seats near the indoor water fountain. After ordering a vanilla latte, she sat down for a rest and a good read. There she sat for quite a long time reading her new mystery. Then she heard someone call her name.

"Melissa?"

She looked up to see a tall, handsome man looking down at her.

Again, he said, "Melissa, is that you?"

"Yes, I'm Melissa Andrews....who are you?"

The man sat down and broke into a smile. Her heart turned over in her chest as she recognized the familiar dimples in his cheeks and the beautiful grey eyes.

"Scott, after all these years, I can't believe it's you!"

"What are you doing up here in the land of the frozen north?" he asked.

"I ran away from home," she replied with a joyful laugh. "What are you doing here?"

"I live here," Scott said. "Let me get a cup of coffee for your runaway woman story...I can't wait to hear it."

When he was again seated, she said, "No, really, I left David. I'm staying at our cottage up at Summer Lake until I decide what to do next."

Scott looked at his cup. "I'm glad you finally woke up....David was always an egomaniac." He flashed her a smile and cleared his throat. "Tell me about yourself. Did you become an art teacher or a famous artist?"

"No, I gave up painting to become a housewife and mother of two children. I didn't work outside the home. It always seemed to be a bad time for me to leave the children and David's needs. I really never amounted to anything except a grandmother."

"Being a grandmother is enough, Melissa. Not every

woman wants a career. Many who try to balance a career and family find it too exhausting and don't do a good job of either. I congratulate you for finding your mission in life."

"I'm not sure about that. But, I'm not sorry for the time I've given to my children and grandchildren. Now, David? That is something else entirely." She sipped her latte and was pensive for a minute.

"I recently discovered he's been running around on me for years....probably from the start, if the truth were known. It shook me to the core when I caught him out with a woman younger than our daughter." She sketched out the details as he sat and listened as though her story was the only one he ever wanted to hear. She decided to end her tale of woe.

"Go figure....I finally made a decision on my own and it was leaving a thirty-five year marriage!" She looked at the fountain, then back at Scott.

"What about you, Scott? Did you ever get through law school?"

"Yes, I graduated with honors and got a job offer from a prestigious corporate law firm here in Ridgewood. I've practiced corporate law forever, it seems. After law school, I married a girl I met here and we have two children, both grown with kids of their own now.

"Mary Ellen and I had a great life together raising the kids. We did a bit of traveling after I retired. She died two years ago from an aneurism. It was sudden and left me wandering around talking to myself. I went back to the office part-time in order to have something to do. It's lonely in the house with her not there."

Melissa fought back tears. "I'm sorry. It must be difficult for you. You know, I've often thought about you over the years and wondered where you were and what you were doing."

"Not much...." Scott laughed and rubbed his face with his hand. "I always thought I would do something meaningful like argue a case before the Supreme Court, but the occasion never arose. Corporate law is basically boring. Say, what are you doing for dinner?"

"Nothing, I'll probably get some take-out food here at the mall before returning home to the cottage."

"Let's go to this little restaurant I know here in the mall. It's so cold and icy outside. If we go there, we can walk to the restaurant under a roof."

"Okay, that sounds like fun....we can talk over the old days." Melissa laughed and handed all her heavy packages to Scott and took his arm just as she had in college.

After a very long walk, requiring them to dodge hundreds of shoppers, they arrived at an Italian restaurant which smelled divine. Scott asked for a corner table where they collapsed and immediately ordered a bottle of wine.

Melissa's cell phone rang and she saw it was David. She reached down and turned it off and returned it to her handbag.

Scott raised his glass and said, "To the old days we spent together."

Melissa looked at him and again, tears came to her eyes. "Don't make me cry, Scott Walker."

They talked about their families and old college days. When she looked at her watch, she was shocked. It was after nine o'clock.

"Scott, it has gotten far too late for me to drive back to the cottage. The roads around the lake have been plowed, but the new snow will hide the road from sight in the dark. I need to find a hotel. Is there one close by?"

"Don't be ridiculous, come to my house. It's about a half hour away and has plenty of bedrooms. Of course, if you stay, you will be a ruined woman since you're married to another man." Scott chuckled as he gathered up her packages.

"You can follow me in your car. Do you still have a heavy foot?"

"Of course." *I can't believe he remembers me driving him around the college campus in my little VW bug with him screaming and pretending fear while I sped around corners howling with laughter.*

At long last, they drove over a small bridge and down a long driveway. When she saw Scott's home, she was overwhelmed. A beautiful two story colonial house nestled in the woods, Christmas candles glowed in the many windows, while spotlights lit the outside. It was a picture waiting to be painted and tears formed in her eyes. *Talk about Currier and Ives....*

Because of the frigid weather, they parked in the garage and dashed into the state-of-the-art kitchen. The room was meant to be homey. A large round wooden table spoke of many shared family meals. It was obvious Mary Ellen had enjoyed cooking and entertaining.

Scott walked ahead of her into the living room where he poured them an after-dinner drink. He turned on the gas fireplace and took a seat in a large leather recliner. Melissa sat on an off-white traditional sofa. An oriental rug gave the décor color while soft neutrals covered the many chairs and walls. The room was a comfortable place to read and talk.

A large Christmas tree stood gracefully in front of French doors which probably accessed a terrace. The twinkling lights of the tree reminded her that Christmas was only one day away. Tomorrow was Christmas Eve.

"Was Mary Ellen an interior designer?" she asked.

Scott shook his head. "No, but she loved to decorate. She had the gift for it. She helped several friends to choose furnishings and fabrics. We both loved this house from the first. Over the many years we've lived here, Mary Ellen improved on the structure by adding a terrace and redoing the bathrooms and kitchen. I love this room, especially," he said. "My daughter Carol and her children decorated the Christmas tree the other night. The grandkids think I should get into the Christmas spirit!"

They sat quietly for a while watching the fire and listening to Christmas carols. Finally, Melissa said, "I have no change of clothes with me. Could you find me something to sleep in?"

"Sure, let's go upstairs and I'll show you to your room."

The guest room was done in ocean blues with a white iron bed. It looked fresh and clean. The dresser was antique white with an ornate gold mirror over it.

Print chairs were nested in front of the windows. The skirted table between them held a lamp and book. The bed was covered in an off-white, hobnail bedspread. The room looked like Martha Stewart had just left.

Melissa laughed with delight, "I may never leave this house!"

Scott smiled and said, "This was our daughter Carol's room. When she married, Mary Ellen redecorated the room for guests. You must be tired....let me get you some pajamas."

She dropped into one of the chairs, barely able to believe what had just happened to her. *Just a few hours ago, I was thinking of going back to Florida. Now, I feel like a teenager with a new boyfriend. This evening was perfect, the food, the conversation and of course, Scott.*

She got to her feet and went into the bathroom. After rummaging around in the drawers, she found a new toothbrush and toothpaste so she could brush her teeth.

She had just come out of the bathroom when Scott returned with a pair of his pajamas.

"Make yourself comfortable," he said softly. The door closed with a gentle click.

She slipped into the pajamas, carefully folding her clothes so they wouldn't wrinkle, and got into bed. Just as she reached for her new book, Scott knocked on the door and brought her a cup of hot chocolate and two cookies.

"See you in the morning; sleep as late as you like,"

he said.

It was so much fun to talk with him again and to have a man interested in me. Not once during the evening did I feel the need to compliment Scott or pretend interest in his career. How refreshing.

Around eight-thirty the next morning, she smelled coffee and bacon. Putting on the robe which was hanging on the back of the bathroom door, she made her way to the kitchen. Scott sat at the wood table drinking coffee and reading the *New York Times.* "Big storm coming late tonight," he said. "We may be snowed in by tomorrow."

"Good lord! I need to leave and get to the lake house while I still can." She took a piece of bacon and poured herself a cup of coffee.

"Why don't we do something exciting?" Scott said. "We could go to New York City or to a ski lodge. It would be fun to be someplace else for Christmas."

"I'm in if it's New York," she said without hesitating. "But, I need to shop for jammies and something to wear."

"Really? Well, okay. Let me make some telephone calls and we'll have lunch in New York City. I know just the place." Scott left the kitchen with a grin on his face.

She finished her coffee, then went upstairs, took a hot shower and dressed in her new red cashmere sweater and black slacks. Looking appropriately festive, she went downstairs to find Scott standing at the foot of the steps with two suitcases.

"I got an extra suitcase which you can use so the desk clerk won't be amused." He laughed as he said it and she burst out laughing too.

"Yeah, I'm much too old to be a lady of the evening!"

Two hours later, they were at the Plaza Hotel in New York City. The hotel was dressed in its holiday finest with beautiful flowers and decorations everywhere. Gigantic silver and gold Christmas balls adorned massive swags of evergreens. Clusters of poinsettias in red, pink and white, decorated the tables and counters.

"So what do you think?" Scott asked when they entered their suite.

She looked around and said, "I feel like Cinderella at the ball; it's absolutely beautiful. Thank you for this." She put down her nearly empty suitcase. "I'm a little worried about how to explain the charge on my credit card," she said with a laugh.

"It's my treat," Scott said. "I represent the Plaza owners and this is one of my perks."

For lunch, they went to a charming restaurant that overlooked the ice skaters at Rockefeller Center. Red scarves flew in the breeze and little children were bundled in colorful jackets and hats.

"A penny for your thoughts," Scott said when she had been quiet for a few minutes.

She smiled at him. "I was remembering my kids ice skating here and how much fun they had. Nice memories."

He reached for her coat and helped her into it. "Let's start back so we can see the holiday displays. There is no place like New York City at Christmas time."

People brushed past them carrying bags of flowers and gifts. It was the day before Christmas and everyone was in a hurry to get home.

"I wonder if we can get tickets to a play?" she said.

"I tried earlier, but all the best plays are sold out," Scott said. "You will need to settle for a good dinner instead."

"That's probably more fun anyway. Going to a play prevents a good leisurely meal. I'm always in a rush eating and afraid I'll be late to the show."

"You need to shop and I have a couple extra items to pick up before Christmas. Why don't we agree to meet back in the hotel lobby at five o'clock and have a drink before dressing for dinner?" Scott suggested.

"Sounds perfect." She gave his hand a squeeze and headed to Sax Fifth Avenue to shop for a dinner dress and other necessary items. At Sax, she found a beautifully cut black dinner dress, an A-line with a softly scooped neck and long sleeves. The only decoration was a small bow on the shoulder of the dress where the cowl neck ended. She loved it.

Next, she chose twinkly rhinestone earrings which would enhance the neckline of the dress. Black high heeled shoes completed the Christmas Eve outfit. She hoped Scott would like the dress and that the earrings weren't too youthful.

For Christmas Day, she chose a red crepe blouse and a black pants suit. The blouse was lovely for a quiet dinner. Satisfied with her purchases, she decided to buy something for Scott.

After searching for quite a while, she selected a lovely red cashmere turtleneck sweater which would look fabulous on him. To go with it, she bought him a clear glass ball music box which housed a replica of the Statute of Liberty. When it was wound up, it played "New York, New York" and snow fell on the statute. It made her laugh. She had the gifts wrapped and headed back to the Plaza.

At five o'clock, she arrived in the hotel lobby and looked around for Scott. When she realized he was not there yet, she sat in one of the lobby chairs and listened to an elderly pianist playing Christmas music. The sign on the piano said his name was John Lindeman and she wondered how many years of practice it took to play so beautifully.

Then she glanced across the lobby and saw Scott walking toward her. Just seeing him made her heart skip a beat.

"Let's go into the lounge, I think it's a bit warmer in there." They sat and talked for a long time. Melissa looked down at her watch and realized they would need to hurry to dress for their dinner reservation.

*****

Melissa put on her new dress and used a bit more make-up than usual. When Scott saw her, he smiled a sly grin.

"Wow! I must be the luckiest guy in New York, tonight. You look beautiful."

She smiled shyly and gave him a kiss on the cheek. *What is wrong with me? I'm a married woman, not a school girl.*

The restaurant was a short taxi ride away. It was a French café, but the tables were far enough apart to allow serious conversations.

Twinkling white lights nestled amidst twigs and evergreens hung about the fireplace mantle. Hurricane shades and candles graced the tables while a large Christmas tree stood aglow in the corner of the room. A roaring fireplace and soft Christmas music completed the enchantment.

They each had wine and Scott ordered an elaborate meal. During dinner, they chatted about their kids and how to handle grown children. Once the meal was over, the waiter brought them dessert which they agreed to share with coffee. Scott looked serious when he put his napkin on the table.

"Are you going to get a divorce?"

She was not expecting to make that decision yet, but after spending twenty-four hours with Scott, it was clear to her that she could no longer live with David. She had made her decision, she just hadn't realized it.

"Yes. My life with him was over when I saw him holding hands with Patricia Copley. If I'm being honest with myself, my marriage has been over for quite some time; I just didn't know it until recently. It's time for me to become a grown-up and make my own decisions."

Scott looked at Melissa with love and listened as she finished.

"I haven't thought of David once since I saw you at the mall and that's odd, because prior to seeing you, I was obsessing about the 'unfaithful' husband. I expect I will have to go through quite a battle over money and property; David does not want a divorce. Worse yet, I'm not sure how my grown children will react to the news. I am hopeful they will support my decision, but either way, I need to do what is right for me."

Scott took her hand and said, "Run away with me. I've always loved you and I always will. Marry me; grow old with me. Our lives could be so good, Melissa. This second chance to be together is a gift we should not throw away."

She was quiet for a few minutes. *What will my children think if I remarry soon after the divorce? Will my friends support my decision to remarry? Do I love Scott enough that other peoples' opinions don't matter?*

Then she looked into Scott's eyes and realized she had made that decision when Scott first smiled at her. David had ended their marriage. She was ready to move on with her life.

Suddenly, she knew she had always loved Scott. She knew Scott would put her first and love her forever. *For years, my thoughts turned to Scott when I tired of David's behavior. Now here he is sitting across from me telling me he loves me. This wonderful man is what I want.*

She removed her hands from Scott's and slowly removed her wedding ring. Then she held Scott's hands in hers once again.

"My Christmas promise to you is I will always love you. I will be with you until God separates us many years from now."

Scott reached into his pocket and withdrew a large diamond ring which he put on her finger. "For Christmas and forever," he said as he leaned across the table and kissed her.

For a few minutes, they sat holding hands and smiling at one another like young lovers. They did not need to speak.

Scott ordered champagne and they toasted their Christmas Promises.

Melissa kissed Scott's hand and knew she could face the future unafraid. Scott would always be beside her providing shelter from life's storms.

They walked out of the restaurant holding hands. She didn't feel the snowflakes or the cold which greeted them; their love insulated them from the rest of the world.

And, with Christmas music playing softly, she walked away from the past and into a bright new future.

About the Author

Bruce Ann Ferguson has written for self-enjoyment for years. *The Christmas Promise* is her first attempt to publish a story. She is currently working on a full length novel, *The Doctor's Wife*, which she hopes to have published in 2017. She lives with her husband in Ponte Vedra Beach, Florida.

Reindeer One

Mark Reasoner

Tim Bradley hated flying on Christmas Eve, but se-
niority ruled. New guys like him were stuck flying on
holidays. He'd much rather be hitting the slopes instead
of walking into the lower level of Atlanta's Hartsfield-
Jackson International Airport. The service entrance, as
Tim thought of it.

Tim would have taken flying a mid-air tanker or
AWACS plane over Afghanistan, like he used to with the
Air National Guard, rather than dealing with the world's
busiest airport on the year's busiest holiday.

But that's how it worked flying for a new airline. Tim
joined Trans-Continental Airways when his old company vanished from the skies. Newbies took the lousy
shifts and unpopular runs.

Hartsfield-Jackson didn't help either. People working for airlines not named Delta ranked somewhere between unclaimed baggage and pond scum.

Some pilots flew over Christmas by choice. It paid
more and some people enjoyed it. Older guys with marriages long flown south and grown kids took Christmas

flights for the extra bucks, and Tim knew of one senior captain who always flew a lousy run up to Burlington, Vermont, on the heels of a Tokyo to Denver flight. Rules required a layover after these long trips and the man had family in New England.

And where was the snow? How could it be Christmas without the white stuff?

As he walked down the corridor, he thought old Ebenezer Scrooge might be on to something when three Delta flight attendants passed him.

"Merry Christmas," one of them said.

They were gone before he could reply. But something didn't connect. He'd seen a splash of green. That wasn't a color Delta wore.

Three Trans-Con colleagues came around a corner.

"Merry Christmas, Timmy," Joe Dalton said, "And it looks like you are out of uniform."

Kenny and Tina, flight attendants flying with Joe and Tim tonight, laughed.

Tim stood there, confused. His uniform was correct. Okay, he was carrying his hat. You didn't wear it inside the terminal.

"I don't know, boss," Kenny said as they walked deeper into the airport, "Maybe he forgot the date."

"Or maybe he forgot to pack his wings," Tina said.

Tim wore his Trans-Continental wings on his jacket's left breast like always.

The chuckles subsided as they went into the lounge. Tucked into the lower level of the T concourse, it wasn't much, but was home for a few minutes.

The room had a few tables with plastic chairs, vending machines and a coffee maker along the wall, alongside an old couch for napping. Everyone used it, even the Delta people. Tonight, there were some United crewmembers, three Delta pilots and an American captain in the room when they entered. They grabbed coffee, arranged chairs and sat down around an empty table.

Tim asked Joe about the uniform comment.

"Well," Joe said, putting his own cup on the table, "Take a look." He pointed to his wings. They were the typical wings surrounding a central icon. Only the icon wasn't Trans-Continental's usual silver colored star super-imposed on the letters T and C. It looked like small branches with green leaves and smaller red berries and a snowflake replaced the star.

"What's this?" Tim asked.

"It's Christmas Eve," Tina said. She wore the same wings.

"And these are the wings we wear on Christmas Eve." Joe said, drinking his coffee.

Kenny put down his cup and pushed back from the table. He struck a dramatic pose with his hand over his heart.

"Oh my God, Captain! He doesn't know! We've got a newbie!"

This got everyone's attention. A Delta pilot came over.

"Well, Captain," the pilot said, "Looks like he'll be monitoring the alternate frequency tonight."

That's when Tim saw the green on the Delta uniform again. He looked closer at the wings. The icon—usually the Delta "widget"—was a Christmas tree. Had he missed something? Was there a special dress code for Christmas?

"Would somebody please tell me what's going on?" Tim asked angrily.

"You haven't flown on Christmas Eve before?" The Delta captain asked as he pulled a chair over to join the group. "No, apparently not," he went on before Tim could answer.

"What's up, Paulson?" Joe said, "You slumming or something?"

"Nice to see you too, Dalton."

"Who's the uninitiated?" The Delta captain pointed

to Tim.

"Tim Bradley," Joe said, and then he waved to indicate the others, "And our cabin crew for tonight, Ken Waxman and Tina Fryer."

The man nodded at the group. "Tony Paulson."

"So, what brings you to our dungeon, Tony?" Joe asked.

"Ground clowns took over our break rooms on A and B."

"Parties?" Tina asked.

"Storage," Tony said. "They've piled all their Toys for Tots donations in the lounges. Can't find enough room to turn around."

"But the Marines are supposed to pick things up later tonight."

Tony cocked his head toward Tim. "Now tell me about this newbie. Think you can get him his wings tonight?"

"I don't know," Joe said, "Weather isn't too bad and I haven't heard if the old guy's been talking to anyone yet."

Kenny joined the conversation, "It's early yet. Though by the time we get back toward the mountains it should be prime time. Hope you'll have Tim on the alternate frequency, Cap'n."

"You can bet on it," Joe answered.

This was ridiculous. Flying on Christmas Eve was bad enough, but now they were making fun and talking around him.

"Would someone PLEASE tell me what in the hell you are talking about!"

The room fell deadly silent. Only the coffee maker's gurgling was heard for a few seconds.

And then everyone laughed. Not hysteria or knee-slapping guffaws, but solid chuckles from everyone in the room.

"My friend," Joe said, "Tonight you just might get

the chance to join a very select few. You might become a member of the Mistle Command. For you just might be able to talk to another great flyer tonight—on the only night he flies."

"And you might win your wings," Tina said, pointing to hers, "Just like us." She wore the same wings as Joe with mistletoe and a snowflake replacing the star, the T and the C.

Tim tried to contain the tantrum welling up. He slid his chair back and sat up straight.

"And WHAT," he asked, "is the 'Missile Command'?" He gave the first word its uncommon pronunciation, with a long 'eye' sound in the second syllable.

"Not 'miss-ILE'," Joe said, "Mistle. As in Mistletoe. See?" He pointed to his wings.

"Or—if you were an Atlanta homeboy—you might become one of Tannen's Bombers, and wear these," Tony pointed to his wings.

"Or be a 'HI-Flyer'," said one of the United crew from across the room.

"So THAT's what y'all are calling yourselves now," Tina said, turning toward the voice, "I wondered. What does it stand for?"

"Holly & Ivy." She came over to the table to let the group see her wings. The icon was an inter-twined sprig of holly and a small ivy branch where the airline's globe normally resided.

"Holly & Ivy, 'H' 'I', HI-Flyers."

Tim slumped in his seat, defeated. Kenny put his arm around Tim's shoulder.

"Cheer up, young man; we all go through this the first time. If you're lucky you'll only go through it once."

"How's that?" Tim asked.

"Well," Tony said, "You just might talk to the old boy." Tim looked at Tony and Joe.

Tony turned to Joe. "He really doesn't have a clue, does he?"

"Apparently not," Joe said, "Want to help us fill him in?"

"Sure," Tony said, "I've got a break until the rest of my crew gets in from Ohio. Where shall we start?"

"Just give him the Reader's Digest version."

Tony slid his chair out a few inches from the table, turned toward Tim and crossed his legs.

"All right, son—short course. When you fly on Christmas Eve, there's someone else flying with you. It's the only night he's out there. If you hear him, see him or talk to him then you become a member. You get to wear these wings."

Tony pointed again to the Christmas tree wings he wore. "And if you have any problems," he continued, "He'll help you out. He will make sure you get there, wherever *there* is."

"Because NO ONE doesn't make it in safely on Christmas eve."

"And don't let those maintenance freaks tell you anything different," Joe added, "They may have to go fix a plane somewhere every Christmas Eve, but everyone still gets home."

"That's' right," Tony went on, "Even the rapid response boys know this. Who do they think makes sure a plane is where they can fix it?"

Tim wondered if he'd stumbled into some alternate universe tonight, or if his usually sane and competent colleagues were secretly replaced by alien creatures trying to suck him in.

I'll wake up, he thought, before it gets too deep. Better play along in the meantime, and get a clue to end this.

"So, who is he?" Tim asked.

Tony looked at him, lowered his head and raised an eyebrow. "Oh, kid," he said, "if you have to ask..."

"Isn't it a sorry state of affairs when young ones don't believe anymore?" Joe asked. They all chuckled.

"Come on," Tim said

"Let's put it this way," Tony answered, "His call sign is Reindeer One."

Flies on Christmas Eve, calls himself Reindeer One, helps everyone make it home, if you hear him you get these wings with holiday icons on them...

Everything led Tim to only one conclusion, but it made absolutely no sense. He looked from Joe to Tony to Tina to Kenny. Their faces were deadly serious. But they couldn't be. He couldn't believe what he heard coming from people who were supposedly adults.

"Are you seriously trying to tell me that I might hear..."

"That's what I'm telling you," Tony answered.

"And," Joe said, "I'm telling you that you will actually be listening for him. Make a note, Mr. Bradley, there's an extra frequency to monitor tonight. Set your box two clicks beyond the Guard frequency."

GUARD was the emergency radio frequency used by pilots for years. It was always monitored and a pilot could call for help anywhere, knowing someone would be listening. The only time a pilot in distress couldn't get a call through was if he wasn't in range of anyone.

"But no one uses that frequency," Tim said, "GUARD isn't even used much anymore."

Joe smiled crookedly and Tina put her hand over her mouth to keep from laughing.

"Tim, you're old enough to have flown on Christmas Eve, why haven't you heard Reindeer One?" Tony asked.

"I'm new with Trans-Con. Never had to fly on the holidays before," Tim said, "At my old carrier, I was senior after a few years."

Tony turned, and said, "Well, then, let me tell you a story. It happened last year and if you HAD been flying—at least over the Southeast—you would be a member and we would not be having this conversation."

He turned to the others, "You all remember that?"

"I still don't believe what Houston center did, patching it all around. Anyway, it was late, and one of our boys was northbound from somewhere in South America headed for Memphis..." Tony told the story, starting with the lightning strike.

Getting struck by lightning usually isn't a big deal for modern airliners. Planes had back-ups and batteries, and even if the strike knocked out all systems, including electric power, the pilots most often held their heading and altitude until the systems could restore themselves. But this wasn't a normal strike.

Delta 4-6-7 flew into a major thunderstorm in the middle of the Gulf of Mexico. Now, with no power, no systems, and wind and turbulence throwing the plane in every direction, the pilots couldn't hold a heading for more than a few seconds. In the middle of dark storm clouds, they couldn't see anything and could only tell if they were holding altitude by the feeling in their seats. The pilot's butt told him they were falling out of the air. The pilot tried calling for help.

"...This is Delta Airlines flight four-six-seven, northbound over the Gulf of Mexico. I am declaring an emergency. This is Delta four-six-seven. I have been struck by lightning; I am in a severe thunderstorm." The pilot released the transmit button and listened for a reply. None came.

"Captain," the co-pilot said, "I think we lost our radio, too."

"... Ta... six-seven. ...Center..." came a static-filled and crackling voice from the pilot's headset, "... up... on...dar. ... Plea... ...peat."

"Try GUARD," the pilot said.

The co-pilot reached over to the radio set. He turned the dial over to the old GUARD emergency frequency. Then he turned it two more clicks and hit his transmit button. "This is Delta four-six-seven. I am declaring an emergency. I repeat—I am declaring an emergency. We have been hit by lightning and have lost all power. Winds and rough air knocking us off course and we can't see to gain heading. We are losing altitude. Emergency, emergency." He lifted his thumb from the transmit button.

His hand went to his left pocket. He touched the wings pinned there. They weren't his usual wings. He wore the ones with the Christmas tree icon.

"Ho, ho, ho," the pilot heard in his headset, "Merry Christmas, Delta four-six-seven. Good to hear from one of Jake's crew." The voice was gruff and deep, but sounded joyous and filled with good cheer.

The pilot's head shot up and his entire body tightened. He looked over at his co-pilot as he pushed his transmit button. "This is an emergency frequency. You are not authorized to be on it," he said. The co-pilot shook his head, smiling, and pointed to the frequency display on the radio. "We're not on GUARD, Captain."

More words came through the headset. "Hear you are having a little trouble. Could we be of service?" The voice was crystal clear and whoever it was spoke as if he was just happy to be talking.

The captain pushed to transmit. "Identify yourself. This is Delta Airlines, flight four-six-seven."

"You can call me Reindeer One," the Delta Captain heard in reply. "I can see you and you are headed northwest. Your heading is two-nine-five." The pilot looked at the co-pilot.

"Reindeer One?" he said.

The co-pilot just smiled and nodded. "Reindeer One, Captain, and he's got our course."

The pilot transmitted again, "Okay, Reindeer One— or whoever you are. If we're headed northwest, where are you?"

"Oh, I'm just behind and above you. Are you headed to Houston?"

"Memphis."

"Well," came the response, "just turn right and head

straight on toward morning." A chuckle came through, "You can set your course zero-one-zero."

The co-pilot asked quietly, "May I?" The captain nodded.

"That's the problem, Reindeer One, we don't have systems yet and we need a little shepherding while things reset. Can you give us a lead?"

"I'd be happy to. I'll come up your port side and lead you on to Memphis. And you might tell your passengers to look out their windows to see me come by."

With emergency power only, there wouldn't be any problem seeing someone fly past the windows. Only the white and red lights along the floor provided any lighting in the cabin. Of course, the pilot couldn't let the passengers know since the intercom was not working either. So only a few passengers saw a red light flying past the port side windows.

One was a Virgin Atlantic flight attendant deadheading back to the states after a few days of vacation in Brazil. She wasn't in uniform, but tucked into her baggage was a pair of Virgin wings with a candle icon. She was a member and when she saw the red-lit aircraft fly by the lurching plane, she smiled and relaxed. Help was here.

Up in the cockpit, the two pilots also saw the aircraft fly past and move into position directly ahead.

"Just follow me," the voice said.

After another minute, lights started coming back on and systems began returning to life. It would take another minute for everything to power back up, but soon the pilots saw they were indeed on course zero-one-zero, and their compass showed they were northbound. They followed their guide out of the storm.

The co-pilot kept a steady conversation with Reindeer One as they flew through the storm. Crossing an imaginary line in the sky, they came out of it with the southern coast line of the United States just ahead.

"Delta four-six-seven, this is Houston center, do you

copy?" They were still on Reindeer One's frequency, but now heard regular air-traffic control.

"We copy," the pilot responded, "Reading five-by-five."

"Welcome back, four-six-seven," Houston responded. "Return to regular channel."

The co-pilot reached over to the radio. Before switching frequencies, he said, "Thanks for your help, Reindeer One."

"Merry Christmas," the other pilot replied.

"...And about half-way through, Houston center patched the conversation to any plane and center monitoring the alternate frequency. I think just about every pilot and flight crew out there heard." Tony took another sip of coffee.

"And I think we got several hundred new members," Tina added. "A couple of my friends heard him and got their wings in January."

Tim stared frozen at Tony. His jaw dropped and his eyes lost focus. Five seconds passed.

"Are you serious?" Tim asked. "Do you really expect me to believe that?"

"I don't expect you to believe or not," Tony replied. "I'm just telling you what happened last year. You can do with it what you want."

Joe looked at his watch and put his cup down.

"Time to go, folks," he said. "Our plane should be in and we need to move."

Tina and Kenny joined Joe. They gathered up cases and topcoats and moved toward the door. Tim left behind them and turned back toward Tony before leaving the room. He just shook his head when Tony smiled.

No one spoke as they walked down the corridor toward the outside door. Leaving the warmth of the terminal behind, they waited outside in the weather for a shuttle bus to take them to their gate.

They could have walked through the terminals, but

that meant going upstairs to the main level, across to the central area, down to the trains, then traveling to D and doing it all over again to their gate. And if their plane wasn't in, they'd stand around with the passengers milling about. Not the smartest thing to do when you were flying the plane. So they stood in the night air waiting on the bus.

It was certainly nicer than the weather in Colorado. Denver had twelve inches of snow on the ground with another two to three inches forecast for Christmas Day. Great for skiing but not anything else without being wrapped up in four layers of down, gore-tex or flannel. Atlanta was forty-five degrees and partly cloudy. Cold for the South, but typical for Christmas Eve.

After a five minute ride across the tarmac, they entered Concourse D and walked up to the main level. The crew ran directly into the swarming mass of humanity that was Hartsfield-Jackson. Christmas Eve could be one of the busiest travel days of the year, and every airport was crowded tonight.

Even if Tim wanted to talk about Tony's story, he couldn't. Not until they were on the airplane itself.

Arriving at their gate, they escaped from the traveling hordes. Joe walked behind the gate counter and picked up the manifest while Ken swiped his ID card and keyed in the access code. The door opened and all four moved into the metal corridor. They walked quickly down the jet way and onto the empty plane.

Ken and Tina stowed their bags just inside the cabin door. They moved across to the galley to sort through the newly loaded drinks, snacks, and other things left behind by the catering crew. Tina signed the paperwork and clipped it to the side of a compartment above the counter. The gate agent would take it with the final paperwork.

Tim and Joe entered the cockpit. Tim went first, stowing his bag and case behind the door. He removed his jacket as he stepped over the seat and lowered himself into his co-pilot's station. He kept moving as Joe was right behind him.

In a minute, they were both seated and started running through the pre-flight checks and inspections. Cockpit settings and checklists came first. Later, before the gate agents started boarding passengers, Joe, Tim or both would leave the cockpit and do a walk-around inspection of the entire plane, checking the landing gear, baggage compartment doors, lights, everything they could see or touch to make sure their plane was in proper order.

If something was wrong, they'd let the ground crew know and wait for things to be fixed or replaced. Or wait for the flight to be cancelled.

Unlikely, as both men knew the ground crews and mechanics took great pride in keeping each plane flying. Their word was more than enough to satisfy any pilot. If they said you could fly, you could fly.

But regulations were regulations and besides, most pilots were superstitious enough to do the walk-around just to make sure. Joe remembered a story about an old lady who asked a pilot why he walked around the plane looking at everything.

"So, we'll get there," the old pilot said.

With thirty minutes to go before boarding began, Tim thought it would be a good time to ask Joe more about Tony's story.

"Joe," he said, "about this Reindeer One thing."

"Not now, Tim," Joe said, "Let's wait until we get to up to cruising altitude. Denver is a long way and it will pass the time."

"But make a note to check on that frequency we talked about when you do the tower check-in and get the weather."

Tim made the note. Two clicks past GUARD, he remembered, not that he believed it—but being the junior member of the crew, AND as his captain was well-known and respected in the flying fraternity, he figured he'd better do as he was told.

An eclectic mix of passengers began to board the plane. Some families, a few college kids with over-stuffed backpacks, a group of older folks dragging shopping bags and wearing fanny-packs and a few business friends with laptop bags slung over shoulders and cell-phones glued to one ear.

Tina and Ken answered questions about service, bags, restrooms, lights, etc. *A lot of travelling rookies tonight.*

Rookies, heck, Tina thought after saying where the restroom was for the fourth time. *Amateurs.*

"I'll be back," Joe said to Tim, leaving the cabin. He could have made Tim do the walk-around but liked to do it himself. He was also superstitious enough to believe the old story.

Tim would have gone along if only to ask about this Reindeer One. But the co-pilot needed to finish the cock-pit pre-flight while his captain was outside.

Things moved quickly. Passengers finally got settled for takeoff, final checks were completed and paperwork finished and signed. Time to get the fully packed metal tube off the ground.

The ground crew hooked their tug to the front wheel and pulled the chocks out. The plane rolled forward a few feet until the little tug's power could counteract several thousand tons of steel, fuel, rubber and humans wanting to roll into the building. Tim loved the feeling. Now we're committed, he thought.

The tug pushed the Boeing 757 back onto the ramp. Joe steered little, letting the ground crew do most of it, and when the plane's nose pointed straight toward the south runways, the ground crew stopped pushing and un-hooked the tug. Joe powered up the engines as the lead ground crew member signaled for him to run up the revs until it sounded right.

Some ground crew guys learned this in the Navy, working on carrier flight decks signaling for catapults to launch. Some, including tonight's guy, would use that style in "launching" planes at Hartsfield-Jackson. They crisply directed planes, pointing and gesturing with panache, and then salute when the plane was ready. Joe smiled as his ground man saluted him and trotted back to the tug.

They rolled out to the taxiway and turned left. Takeoff was to the west tonight, into Atlanta's usual winter wind. Joe and Tim taxied down the taxiway toward the end of the runway. Tim clicked on the intercom and announced takeoff.

"Good evening and Merry Christmas from the cockpit, ladies and gentlemen," he said. "And we'd like to add our welcome aboard. We're number two for takeoff and so I'd like to ask the flight attendants to prepare the cabin. Thanks again for flying Trans-Continental."

"Remember the alternate frequency," Joe said.

"Yes, sir," Tim said. "You're the boss."

Joe chuckled as he turned the 757 onto the runway proper. "Oh, don't worry," he said, "I'll tell you the story as soon as we get the bird up and settled."

The engines throttled up. Joe released the brakes and the big jet rolled down the runway gathering speed. The nose wheel came off the ground and then came the most magical moment of any flight.

A jet's engine momentum sent it those first few feet into the air after the nose came up, following one of Sir Isaac Newton's laws. After that, the plane settled onto its cushion of air, forgetting Newton and following Mr. Bernoulli's principles.

It felt like the plane was gently falling back down. A person felt it as their body settled into the seat bottom and the plane rose into the air.

The first part of any flight was busy in the cockpit as

the plane rose to cruising height and proper course, so Tim had no chance to bring up Reindeer One. But soon announcements were made and instruments set, and Tim could finally ask the question eating him. He would not let this flight end without an answer.

Joe sensed Tim's anxiety and smiled. He remembered first learning about Reindeer One. Of course, he didn't just learn about the other flyer that night, he actually talked to him. Joe knew he'd tell the story to Tim, but wanted to drag it out.

Pilots only get to have this fun once a year, he thought.

"So what do you want to know?" Joe finally asked.

Tim didn't reply for a few seconds. Finally, he said, "I want to hear the story."

"Which one?" Joe asked. "I've got three. There's my story, the basic story, and Jake's."

"Jake's?" Tim asked.

"Jake's it is," Joe said.

Tim probably didn't want to hear Jake Tannen's story, Joe thought, *but so what? There would be time to tell the others. Lots of time to fill up here tonight.*

"My friend," Joe began, "Jake's story is THE story. Jake Tannen was the first pilot to talk with Reindeer One on Christmas Eve. Or at least the first to admit it publicly."

Joe stretched out his arms, scanned the instrument panel one more time and got comfortable. He told Jake's story.

****

Jake was one of the first jetliner pilots for Delta Airlines. He flew some of the first coast-to-coast flights, and flew some of the first Boeing 707's to come off the line. He didn't mind flying on holidays, Jake figured people needed to get home—or wherever they needed to go— and flying was flying.

One Christmas Eve, back about fifty years ago, Jake was flying from New York to San Francisco. The weather was lousy everywhere, and flights were being cancelled left and right.

Jake took off around nine o'clock for what should have been a five-hour flight. With time zones, that would have put him into San Francisco about eleven o'clock local time. Things didn't work out as planned. He fought a headwind most of the way and somewhere over Missouri; things went from bad to worse.

Though the Boeing Company assured everyone these new planes could stand up to anything Mother Nature could throw, save for a hurricane, pilots and passengers weren't so tough. Flying through a storm could throw everyone around, not to mention drinks, meals, books, suitcases and anything not bolted down.

And that's what happened as Jake tried to plow through a nasty blizzard throwing everything it had at the Midwest. The plane bounced up and down, left and right, and though Jake made the passengers and flight attendants strap themselves in, things still rocked, rattled and rolled.

Then the lightning hit. A Boeing 707 was rated to survive a lightning strike, and this one did, but the electrical systems weren't so lucky. The cockpit lights went out and Jake knew the cabin was in the dark too. A few seconds later, the emergency systems kicked in and some light was restored along with some instruments.

Jake glanced at the crucial readings. The compass still functioned, reading something, but who knew what? Lightning could destroy magnetism. The pressure-driven altimeter showed the plane maintaining altitude.

That was good, Jake thought.

There was nothing outside the window showing motion of any kind, just a vast dark gray expanse, interrupted by lightning flashes and ice particles hitting the window.

The flight engineer reported all engines functioning, though number three was starting to run hot. Jake told him to keep an eye on it and shut the engine down if it hit the red zone.

The flight crew could hear the flight attendants trying to calm everyone. Jake smiled. Everyone was in it together.

He needed to let someone know what happened, but heard only muted humming through the headphones.

"This is Delta Flight two-oh-seven calling any tower, any control."

Silence.

Okay, try another frequency. He figured maybe they'd passed into the Kansas City control area or Oklahoma City to the southwest. So he looked up both and tried again.

"Kansas City control, this is Delta two-oh-seven, over." Nothing. He switched over.

"OKC, this is Delta two-oh-seven, come in." Still nothing.

No need to panic just yet, the plane was still flying, and heading in a generally correct direction.

The co-pilot heard Jake calling and getting no response.

"Captain?" the co-pilot asked, "Is there a problem?"

"You mean other than the obvious?" Jake replied.

****

"So there they were," Joe said, "Somewhere over the heartland with no radio contact, few instruments and fewer choices."

"Why didn't he fly a triangle pattern, like the Brits do?" Tim asked.

"Nice to see you know your history, young man," Joe said with a grin.

In World War II, the RAF devised a last-ditch procedure for planes without radio, instruments or chances for the pilot to bail out. The process called for the pilot to fly left-handed triangles in hopes some tower or radar station would notice and send up another plan to "shepherd" them home.

The procedure was still recognized today, though little used as it was unusual for any legitimate flight to go completely off the grid or be unidentified.

"He might have, if his next option hadn't worked," Joe said, picking up the story.

****

There was one more radio option. If they had any power and were transmitting at all, then the GUARD frequency might help. GUARD was a pilot's last resort in an emergency. It was always monitored and declaring an emergency got noticed. So Jake changed to the GUARD frequency.

Or so he thought. Jake actually set his radio dial past GUARD. Two clicks past to be exact.

"Emergency, emergency, this is Delta Flight two-oh-seven calling any tower, any control center."

"Merry Christmas," replied a voice. It didn't sound like a usual controller.

Great, Jake thought, I get some idiot hanging out in Podunk tower celebrating Christmas with his eggnog and listening to chatter. *This guy will be a lot of help.*

But at least someone was hearing him, so he might as well try to get help.

"Whoever you are," Jake said, "I have an emergency. This is Delta Flight two-oh-seven and I have no electric power, no position."

"Well," the voice said, "How can we help you?"

Jake didn't know where to start, there were so many things wrong. Before he could answer, the voice came back.

"Could we guide you to somewhere?"

"How about an airport?" Jake answered. He really didn't think whoever he was speaking to could help, but it was something to focus on.

"Any place in particular?" came the reply. "Things are very nice up north where I'm from."

"Where's that?" Jake asked.

"Ho, ho, ho," the voice said, "I'm sure it's a lot farther north than where you're flying. Where are you headed, my friend?"

Jake looked at his co-pilot, who stared blankly out the window, and then at his flight engineer. The engineer looked at his own console.

"Any opinions, gentlemen?" he asked.

"Um, well, Captain," the co-pilot ventured, "I guess we can at least ask. Whoever this guy is, he's the only person we've talked to since we got hit."

"What do you think?" Jake asked the flight engineer. He shrugged.

Jake keyed his mike again, "Okay. Whoever you are, we'll take any help you can give us."

"By the way," Jake continued, "Who are you?"

"Just call me Reindeer One."

Jake looked at his crew. Neither man reacted.

"Uh, roger, Reindeer One," Jake said. "We are supposed to be headed to San Francisco International, but we need to put down safely wherever we can."

"Well, then," the voice said, "Let's head west. I'm going that way too, so I can lead you."

A red light streaked past the co-pilot's window, taking position dead ahead at their same altitude.

"Follow on, my friends," the voice said.

For the next hour, Jake and his crew worked to reestablish contact with any tower, field or other airplane while following their guide. They brought some power back by using batteries and APUs, but that only gave them the intercom and limited lighting in the cabins.

****

"Just like that," Tim said, "Some magical appearance by another flyer that just happened to be in the right place with all the right information. I don't believe it, Captain."

"I'm just telling you the story, Tim," Joe replied.

"Sure," Tim said.

Joe picked up the story again.

Every fifteen minutes, Jake switched to other frequencies to raise any tower or control center. He had no luck.

"We're coming out of the storm," the voice said after another hour passed. "Can you see the lights down there?"

"Affirmative," Jake replied.

"That's Sacramento," the voice said, "And if you stay with me, I'll take you down to the San Francisco approach."

Jake landed without incident, though he had a lot of explaining to do once the passengers were de-planed and everything secured.

"I still don't believe it," Tim said after Joe finished the story.

"Neither did the authorities at the time," Joe said, "Tannen and his crew spent most of the next week explaining what happened."

"Why didn't they just check the cockpit recorder?" Tim asked, "Oh, I know. It was magical, and the conversation mysteriously didn't record."

Joe smiled at the sarcasm.

"Actually," Joe said, "They didn't think of it. By the time someone did, the plane was back in service and the conversation recorded over."

"You mean the FAA and everyone just took his word?

"Not really, they investigated and found a couple of HAM operators who confirmed the conversation between Delta two-oh-seven and Reindeer One. After that, they dropped the matter."

"Did they ever find out who the guy really was?" Tim asked.

"Sort of," Joe said. "The next Christmas, Jake was flying from Boston to Los Angeles, when Reindeer One surfaced again."

That Christmas, an American Flight had to be shepherded from Chicago to New York City. An engine had caught fire over upstate New York and they were trying to get down in one piece.

Jake heard their distress call and tried that frequency. He didn't have to do anything, as Reindeer One was already talking to the plane in trouble. Jake just announced his presence and asked if they could help.

"American fifteen-seventy, this is Delta three-eight-five. Can we be of assistance?"

"Well hello, Captain Tannen." It was that voice again.

"I think we can take this broken eagle home. Thanks for the offer."

"No problem, Reindeer One," Jake replied, "Good luck, American."

"Fifteen-seventy not only made it safely, the Idlewild tower heard the conversation too," Joe continued.

"Idlewild?" Tim asked.

"Sorry," Joe said, "That's the old name for JFK. Anyway, Captain Tannen was called before another inquiry, but he supported the American pilot's story, and since the tower heard it too, the FAA chalked it up to good flying and good luck. Whoever Reindeer One was, he hadn't done anything wrong."

"Why didn't this ever become public?" Tim asked.

"Are you serious? Do you have any idea how the public would have reacted? This was the sixties, Tim, and there were still some things people were better off not knowing."

"But pilots believed it?" Tim said.

"Pilots are a superstitious lot, my friend," Joe said. "You should know that."

"Anyway," he continued, "after that, pilots in trouble started trying the other frequency to raise Reindeer One on Christmas Eve.

Tim shook his head and looked back to the instruments. Everything was as it should be. Then he looked out the window at the darkness. There were lights below, but the plane was too high to make out many details.

Captain Dalton gave a new order to his co-pilot.

"Mr. Bradley, inform Memphis center we are changing to the alternate frequency for five minutes."

Tim looked at his captain.

"Do it, co-pilot," Joe said.

Tim did as he was told. Memphis center acknowledged without question. Tim changed his radio and immediately heard chatter.

"No word from the old boy yet, ASA. But it's still early."

"Roger, US seven-three. We'll be checking as we head east."

Tim announced his presence. "This is Trans-Continental thirty-one-fifty-five, westbound from Atlanta to Denver at 31,000 feet."

"Good evening, Trans-Con. This is ASA forty-eight seventy-six eastbound from Houston to Hartsfield-Jackson at twenty-five thousand. No contact with Reindeer One reported."

"Copy, ASA; we're going to listen in for a few minutes."

"Roger," the other pilot said. "It may be quiet, though."

It was. There was no more conversation until Joe had Tim sign off and switch back to the Memphis frequency. The controller asked if there was any conversation with Reindeer One.

"Uh, negative, Memphis," Tim said.

"Roger, Trans-Con, understood," the Memphis controller replied.

Tim took down a new weather forecast and updated his own systems with the data from Memphis. Then he signed off.

The next air traffic control center was Kansas City. Tim checked in with them while Joe called the cabin to tell the flight attendants he was coming out of the cockpit.

"Save your questions, Tim," he said, getting up. "I'll be back."

****

Joe locked the door behind him. Current security procedures required the re-enforced cockpit door remain locked at all times. No one wanted terrorists or other bad guys getting access to the controls.

But pilots still had to take care of business. Such was the case now.

After completing his business, Joe talked with Ken and Tina.

"Any problems?" He asked.

"No, sir," Tina said. "Everything seems to be going smoothly."

"Well, except for the squealer in row thirty-four," Ken said, referring to a screaming infant back in coach.

"How are things up front?" Tina asked. "Heard anything?"

"It's quiet," the captain replied.

"Speaking of which," Ken said, "have you told Tim the story?"

"Uh-huh," Joe said. "But he doesn't believe it."

Ken laughed and said, "Don't blame him. I didn't believe it either when I heard Reindeer One the first time. But then I got my wings and heard the whole story."

Ken Waxman first heard Reindeer One talking to

a plane in distress five Christmases ago. His pilot was monitoring the alternate frequency and listened to Reindeer One help a cargo flight out of Detroit fly safely across Lake Ontario into Buffalo when the plane's radar malfunctioned. The pilot called back to the flight attendants and let them listen in.

Ken hadn't understood what he'd heard until his wings came in January. Then he asked another pilot about Reindeer One. The other pilot told Ken the whole story and also told him to wear those wings on Christmas Eve.

Joe returned to the cockpit and strapped himself into his seat. Tim gave him a quick status report. All was well.

"Is that it?" Tim asked.

"No," Joe replied, "that was the beginning. As the years passed, pilots and controllers began to monitor the frequency and if they got into trouble, called for Reindeer One's help."

"Some pilots would even go there just to talk to the old guy,"

"How did that work out?" Tim asked.

"Hit and miss," Joe said. "The old guy loves to talk to other flyers, but won't take the time unless a plane needs help. And then, of course, there are the wings."

"Yeah, what about the wings?" Tim said.

"They started showing up after fifteen-seventy's encounter," Joe said, "Jake Tannen got a small package in the mail with a set of pilot wings like the one my friend Tony was wearing tonight. The note simply recalled the encounter and said Jake might enjoy a small souvenir. All of the other crew members got wings, too."

"Jake and his colleagues wore them on the next Christmas Eve," Joe continued, "as did the American crew."

"What did their wings look like?" Tim asked.

"Two candles where the two A's normally go. Eventually, every airline had a special set for anyone who talked with Reindeer One."

"Does Reindeer One also give you the name?" Tim asked.

"No, that's our doing," Joe said. "Just a way to feel a little more connected to others who have them."

"Captain, I'm sorry," Tim said. "But with all due respect, I do not believe a word of this. It sounds like something out of Operation Blue Book or Area 51."

"Don't forget Cheyenne Mountain," Joe chuckled.

Tim rolled his eyes and groaned. "Oh, come on,"

"I'm serious." Joe turned to face the window. He didn't want to show Tim the smile breaking out on his face.

"Haven't you ever heard of NORAD's Santa Tracker?"

"That's just Air Force P.R.," Tim replied.

"Is it?" Joe asked, turning back to his co-pilot. After a few seconds, he couldn't hold the straight face and laughed.

"You're right," he said. "It is. But trust me; the folks there do know about Reindeer One. After all, they monitor everything in the airspace."

"And besides," Joe continued, "there has to be something to it, when you consider the history."

"How so?" Tim asked.

"You know, Mr. Bradley," Joe said, "if this was a training flight, or a check ride, I'd give you a homework assignment. But since it's not, let me pose this simple question."

"How many plane crashes, or even almost-crashes, do you know of happening on Christmas Eve?"

Tim thought for a few moments.

"Come on, Tim," Joe said. "You know your history. Your comment about the British shepherd procedure proved that."

"Not really," Tim said. "I just remember reading Frederick Forsyth's book."

Joe smiled. He knew the book. Most pilots did, or at least knew the story.

Tim still didn't answer the question.

"The answer, my young friend," Joe said, "is none. Zero. There has never been a fatal commercial airplane crash on Christmas Eve since the industry started flying through the night."

"Seriously?" Tim asked.

"Seriously," Joe said. "Look it up if you don't believe me."

"And you're saying it's all because of this mysterious but ever-present Reindeer One?"

"No, Tim, I'm not saying that," Joe said. "I'm simply noting an historical fact. There have never been any fatal crashes in our business on Christmas Eve."

"Reindeer One is a separate story," he said. "One that you asked for, by the way."

"I'm starting to wish I hadn't," Tim said.

"It's all right," Joe said, "Most un-initiated pilots have similar reactions. Even me."

"You've done this too?" Tim asked.

"I'm wearing the wings," Joe said. "So, yes, I've talked to Reindeer One. And not just talked to him. The old boy saved me and my airplane."

"Really?"

"Yes, really," Joe replied. "Would you like to hear it?"

"Might as well," Tim said, "We've still got time."

Before Joe told his story, he and Tim took care of some regular duties. They checked in with the various towers on their route. While this trip would have them in communication with four area control centers, Atlanta, Memphis, Kansas City and finally Denver, they still needed to check in with airport towers along the way. It helped to keep them out of the way of the local air traffic, and kept them up-to-date on changing weather conditions and such.

Tonight, it gave them more chances to ask if Reindeer One was broadcasting.

The alternate frequency was still silent, though Kansas City reported the old guy was heard by a trans-Atlantic flight headed into Boston's Logan Airport.

With everything updated and reset, Joe told Tim his story.

"I had my first conversation with Reindeer One just over twenty years ago. I was working for a rich guy down in Texas, flying his Gulfstream around everywhere."

"You were a private pilot?" Tim asked.

"Corporate," Joe said, "though it was really one and the same. This guy owned several companies. He was into oil & gas, real estate, cattle and who knows what else. Most of the time I flew him to meetings and inspections all over the country. I also flew his family around and got to visit some neat places that way."

"The only downside," Joe continued, "was I gave up my holidays to fly my boss wherever he wanted to celebrate. The guy didn't spend a single Christmas or New Year's at home in all the years I worked for him. And when I wasn't flying him or his people, I flew for charity."

"Charity?" Tim asked.

"Haven't you heard of the Corporate Angels?" Joe asked.

"Yes," Tim answered. "They work with cancer patients."

"That they do," Joe said. "And I did some of those flights. But there were others, too."

"Sometimes patients and doctors are needed somewhere in a hurry, and so a corporate jet would arrange to take them. This one was set up by a heart surgeon who knew my boss."

"I was flying from Houston to Indianapolis that Christmas Eve, with the doctor, his patient and her family. My boss and his family were also along. We were dropping the doctor and patient in Indy, and then heading on to New York."

"The patient was a ten-year old girl who needed a heart. The organ was waiting in Indianapolis, still beating inside the body of a brain dead shooting victim. Things couldn't last forever, and the doctors thought it easier to bring the still living kid to Indiana, rather than trying to remove the heart and fly it to Houston."

"Anyway," Joe continued, "having committed to taking the folks, we were on a really tight schedule. My boss and his family came on board first and once the others were loaded and strapped in, we were set. Things started to go south almost before we could get airborne."

****

I taxied out to the runway and radioed for permission to take off. The tower advised me weather was moving in later, particularly over the Midwest and Northeast. Fast falling temperatures could lead to major fog and much reduced visibility. But we were committed. Donated organs have a short shelf life and the young child strapped into our cabin desperately needed the one waiting at our first destination.

We had to get her to Indiana University Hospital before midnight. Otherwise the waiting heart would expire, and probably the young girl with it. The doctor was along to assist with the transplant.

So, we went.

The fog started to roll in over St. Louis and on into the Midwest about the time we were over Arkansas.

"Of course, at twenty-five thousand feet you don't really notice ground fog," Joe said.

Tim chuckled. He knew that as well as his captain. It's a reason pilots needed to stay in touch with control centers and airport towers throughout a flight.

We were cruising right along, making really good time. When we passed over Southern Missouri, or at least what we thought was that area, Kansas City center told us to check in with Lambert Field.

"What's going on?" I asked KC.

"Things are deteriorating rapidly, November two-seven," they said.

Most airports in the Midwest were shutting down because of poor visibility. I changed the frequency to Lambert and asked for an update. They asked my position and speed.

"Roger, Gulfstream November two-seven, Recommend you divert here immediately and at best possible speed. You should be able to land before we have to shut down."

"What does it look like to the east?" I asked.

"Not good. Minneapolis is the only airport still open. We're expecting to cease flight operations at about 2300 hours."

That wasn't going to work.

"Thanks, Lambert, we'll try something else."

They acknowledged and I switched back to Kansas City. I told them what Lambert said and asked for a weather update and alternatives.

"Wait one," they said.

We flew in silence for a couple of minutes. I began to think this wasn't going to work. We had enough fuel to go on to New York, and it looked like we could outrun the fog bank if we had to. But there was our patient.

"Gulfstream November two-seven," Kansas City finally said, "We understand St. Louis-Lambert advised you to land there. We recommend that to be your best course. Second option; you may want to divert to here or head back home if you have the fuel."

"Acknowledged, Kansas City," I said, "But we can't do it. We have a medical situation and need other options. We're transporting a critically ill young girl along with her doctor and family to Indianapolis for transplant surgery. We need that field or somewhere close."

"Understood," they said. There was more silence. After about another minute, they came back on.

"Gulfstream November two-seven, we don't have any additional recommendations. We're going to hand you over to Indianapolis center. They're closer to your problem and might have more options. We'll be monitoring and will forward any new information."

"Roger, Kansas City," I answered.

"Two more things," they said. "Lambert Field just informed us the fog moved in faster than expected. You wouldn't have made it anyway."

At least I called that one right, I thought.

"Second," they went on, "Be sure to check the alternate. Best of luck, two-seven, Kansas City out."

"The alternate?" What in the world is that?" I asked my co-pilot.

"It's another option, skipper," the co-pilot said. "Haven't you heard of it?"

I hadn't and said so.

"It might be worth a try," he told me. "I've never used it, but I know guys who have and they say it's bailed them out of jams up here."

I didn't know what to think, but I did know we would start running out of options if I didn't make a decision quick.

"Unfortunately, Tim," Joe said, "I couldn't just make a command decision. It wasn't like this flying where I can decide what to do to save the plane and passengers. I had my boss to consider and more importantly, the girl and her family. I needed to check with them.

"That's what I did next. First, though, I had my co-pilot switch our radio and check in with Indianapolis. Then I went to the cabin to talk with my boss and the others."

"Sir," I said to my boss, "We need to talk. We have a situation developing."

I told him about the fog and the airports. I said we

could make New York but might not be able to get our other passengers to Indianapolis that night.

"That's a problem, son," he said. Before he could say more, the doctor came over.

"I heard a little of what you said, Captain," the doctor said. "What's happening?" I filled him in.

"Captain Dalton," the doctor replied, "my patient may not survive long enough to get back to Indianapolis, or anywhere to get a new heart. And the organ we want to use won't last either. Something else needs to be done."

"I'm trying, sir," I told him. "But there aren't many choices."

Before any of us could say more, the co-pilot called me back to the cockpit. As I moved forward, my boss gave me a parting word.

"Figure something out, Joe," he said. "A lot of people are counting on you."

"Skipper," the co-pilot said as I sat down and strapped in, "I might have some help for us. Remember the alternate KC mentioned?"

"I remember."

"I've got him or at least someone on that frequency. Go two clicks beyond GUARD."

I didn't take time to argue. I identified myself and our flight and asked for a reply. I got one immediately.

"Ho, Ho, Ho, Merry Christmas," I heard in my headset. "I didn't expect to see anyone else flying on this gray and gloomy night."

That was not what I expected to hear.

"What is this?" I asked my co-pilot. "Some goof-ball with an illegal radio? We need assistance, not some joker."

"Just talk to him, Joe," the co-pilot said. "I think he can help. I explained our situation and he says he can guide us to Indianapolis."

I keyed my microphone. "This is Gulfstream November Two-Seven. Who am I talking to and what is your status?"

"Call me Reindeer One. And I'm flying just off your starboard side at your altitude. Can you see me?"

We looked out the right side and sure enough, there were red lights keeping pace with us just far enough away to keep me from panicking.

"We can see you," I said.

"Wonderful. We'll just stay on this course and then I'll guide you down. I understand you have a little one on board looking for a very special Christmas present."

"You could say that."

The course matched our flight plan and should have taken us right to Indianapolis. Not that we'd know, since we couldn't see anything below.

Not knowing what else to try, we followed him. I changed back to Indianapolis and told them we were headed there.

"Sorry, November two-seven," they told me. "Our field is closed. We can't take you."

"I'm declaring an emergency," I told them. I explained our situation.

"We're aware, Kansas City informed us. Ceiling and visibility are zero here. We may not be able to steer you in."

"Roger, Indianapolis," I said. "Am in contact with another pilot who indicates he can bring me there."

"Please confirm your last, two-seven; we have no other pilots on our channels."

That's when I remembered the frequency I talked with Reindeer One on. Two clicks beyond GUARD. I didn't think they would believe me. I paused before answering. My co-pilot sensed my confusion.

"He's still with us, skipper," my co-pilot said. "And we were just talking with him."

I took a breath and told Indianapolis the frequency we were using.

"Understood, two-seven, we'll monitor."

A few seconds later, Reindeer One called again.

"Well now, my friends," he said. "We're going to turn around to the southwest and come down to about ten thousand feet. I'll take the lead and we'll line up for the runway. Follow me."

"Uh, roger, Reindeer One," I said. "But I better let my passengers know." The reply was that joyful chuckle again.

I went back to the cabin and told everyone to strap in tightly. I also told my boss and the doctor what we were trying.

"I don't know who this guy is," I said. "But Indianapolis control is monitoring the situation and I'll abort the landing if I don't feel it's safe."

"However," I went on, "if anyone thinks I'm putting their lives at risk, tell me now. I'll stop this and we'll try something else."

"Captain," the doctor said, "if there's a chance we can land safely, please take it. I gave up this Christmas to give my patient a chance to see next Christmas."

"That's when I knew I had to try, Tim," Joe said. "I could always bail out if I didn't think it was safe or if I saw something. But still..."

"How could you be sure this voice would guide you in safely?" Tim asked.

"I didn't. For all I knew he'd drop me into the Speedway infield or brush me off against the circle monument. But I felt I had to take the chance."

"Anyway...," Joe continued.

I went back to the cockpit. My boss followed. He said he wanted to watch and listen. I couldn't stop him, since it was his plane. He buckled himself in the jump seat and put on an extra headset. I strapped in and got ready to make the turn.

"Reindeer One," I called, "ready to turn and descend."

I told my co-pilot to give me speed and altitude every thousand feet after we came down to ten thousand. Then I let Indianapolis know the plan.

"We copy, November two-seven. Will respond only if requested or needed."

We started a slow turn and descent. It wasn't unfamiliar to any pilot going into Indianapolis International. We came in from the northeast over the Speedway, west of the downtown area. This night, though, I was trusting luck and my guide since we couldn't see anything on the ground.

"It's a normal landing, my friends," Reindeer One said as we hit ten thousand feet. "Just stay with me."

The co-pilot started calling altitude and speed as we went into our approach. The Indianapolis tower gave distance a couple of times; also saying we were right where we should be.

"Five thousand feet. Speed normal."

"Four thousand."

"Three."

"One-quarter flaps," I said. My co-pilot confirmed the flaps.

"Two thousand."

"Three miles from the runway," the tower radioed.

"One thousand feet, skipper," the co-pilot said. "Speed coming down."

"Landing gear," I called.

"Gear down," my co-pilot confirmed. "Landing flaps?"

"Landing flaps."

I had strong grips on the yoke and the throttles. I told my co-pilot to start giving me altitude every one hundred feet and be ready to retract the flaps and the gear if I aborted the landing.

At five hundred feet, and only about a mile from the runway, I still couldn't see anything outside the window. Just gray mist and those red lights in front of the plane.

"Co-pilot," I said, "if we get to one hundred feet and

can't see anything, I am going to abort. Be ready to retract the gear and flaps."

"Understood, Captain," he said.

I told the tower the same thing.

"We copy, two-seven," they said. "Be advised, emergency vehicles standing by. Did you request an ambulance?"

I smiled. "That's affirmative. We are expected."

"Three hundred feet, Captain."

"Two hundred," the co-pilot said, and then called, "There! Lights! I can see the runway."

He was right. We could just see the blue runway lights. And we were headed straight down the middle of them. We passed over the threshold less than thirty feet up. I set the plane down on the tarmac, throttled back and the co-pilot worked the brakes. We came to a stop about three-quarters down the runway.

I glanced up ahead to see if our guide was still in front of us. All I saw were two red lights rocketing upward into the fog.

But I couldn't let him go without saying something.

"Reindeer One, this is Gulfstream November Two-Seven," I called. "Thanks for the help. We owe you one."

"Merry Christmas, my friends."

"Welcome to Indianapolis, Gulfstream two-seven," the tower radioed. "Nice landing. Please return to regular channel."

I turned around to see my boss smiling. He'd heard every word.

"Heckuva job there, son," he said.

Two emergency vehicles pulled up beside us. One was an ambulance and one of the attendants got out and came toward the aircraft door. My co-pilot got out of his seat and followed my boss back to open the door.

As the ambulance crew got the little girl and her parents ready for their ride, the doctor came up to me.

"I told them we were going to try this," he said, "But

it was a big chance. The parents were a little scared, but the little girl told me she was up for it."

"I'm glad we made it," he said.

All I could do was nod. I was glad, too.

"And that's it," Joe said. "The girl made it to the hospital and the transplant was successful."

"And nothing happened after that?" Tim asked.

"Well, I had to file a report, which I did the next morning. My boss and his family decided to fly on the next day on a regular flight. I had to stay around for an investigation after I submitted my report, but I flew the plane on to New York in time for New Year's."

"Anything ever happen about that landing?"

"Not a thing," Joe said. "I only got one question from the investigators and that was to confirm the frequency. That was it. I never heard another word from them."

"I got my wings a little while later. They showed up a couple of weeks into January. My co-pilot and my boss got them, too."

"They're not these wings, Tim," Joe went on. "These came after I signed on with Trans-Con. Those other wings had a different icon. An angel."

Tim shook his head and turned to his instruments. It was simply too much to absorb, let alone believe.

Joe sensed this and spoke again.

"Tim, look," he said. "I can't tell you what to believe or not believe. All I can tell you is what I've experienced and what I've learned."

"You may not believe my story or anything else you've heard tonight, but I can introduce you to a young lady who's living proof."

Joe looked directly at his co-pilot, "Living because Reindeer One brought me in safely in all those years ago."

"And those wings, by the way? I sent them to her when I signed on here and got these."

Tim looked at his captain.

"That's right," Joe said, "The girl's still alive. I've stayed in touch with the doctor over the years, and he's kept me up-to-date. Last we heard, she's married and living in North Carolina."

"I still don't believe it," Tim said. "It just sounds too fantastic."

"Maybe so," Joe replied, "but it doesn't mean it's any less true."

"Okay," Tim said. "Even if I admit this is plausible, where's the proof? I know you've got a story, and I know the cabin crew backs you up, but how do I know you guys aren't just pulling a good joke on the new kid? Where's this Reindeer One tonight? Why hasn't anyone heard him?"

"I don't know, Tim," Joe said. "But I don't need to. I've learned a few other things over the years about the old guy. And there's a couple you can count on."

"What are they?" Tim asked.

"First," Joe said, "If you stay in this business, particularly if you keep flying with Trans-Con, you're going to fly a lot of Christmas Eves. And Reindeer One will, too.

"And second: Someday you'll talk with the old guy. With a little luck, it'll be just because you can. But if not, if you need help up here, Reindeer One will be there for you. That's a promise."

"Understand?"

Tim nodded.

"Alright then," Joe said, turning back to face his controls and windshield, "Why don't you contact Denver Approach and let's start getting this bird ready to land."

Snow began to fall outside, but not so much to cause problems....

About the Author

Mark Reasoner is a Hoosier by birth, a teacher by profession and a storyteller by nature. His writings have appeared in Folio Weekly, the DeKalb Literary Arts Journal and corporate publications. As a software trainer, he develops and narrates computer-based training sessions. He lives and writes in Neptune Beach, Florida.

AI
d